D0190278

MEN'S BAKING MANUAL

AUTHOR'S ACKNOWLEDGEMENTS

That's first and foremost to my wife, Kate and my daughter, Matilda, for being such good cake tasters. Thanks too to Louise McIntyre and all the team at Haynes for doing such a great job on the book. My thanks to Antony Topping and Claudia Young, my agents at Greene & Heaton. Thanks to Fraser Parry and Sue Townsend for help with the photography. Finally thanks you, the reader, for buying this book. You're going to buy it aren't you? Of course you are… it's about cakes and bakes!

© Andrew Webb 2015

All rights reserved. No part of this publication may be reproduced, stored in a retrieval system or transmitted, in any form or by any means, electronic, mechanical, photocopying, recording or otherwise, without prior permission in writing from the publisher.

First published October 2015

A catalogue record for this book is available from the British Library

ISBN 978 0 85733 833 4

Library of Congress control no. 2015936054

Haynes Publishing,
Sparkford, Yeovil, Somerset BA22 7JJ, UK
Tel: +44 (0) 1963 442030
Fax: +44 (0) 1963 440001
E-mail: sales@haynes.co.uk
Website: www.haynes.co.uk

Haynes North America, Inc.,
861 Lawrence Drive, Newbury Park,
California 91320, USA

Printed in the USA by Odcombe Press LP,
1299 Bridgestone Parkway, La Vergne, TN 37086

Author	Andrew Webb
Project manager	Louise McIntyre
Designer	James Robertson
Copy editor	Ian Heath
Indexer	Dean Rockett
Photography	Fraser Parry
	shutterstock.com
Home Economist	Sue Townsend

MEN'S BAKING MANUAL

From puddings to patisserie, sourdough to sausage rolls

Andrew Webb

Contents

| 00 | INTRODUCTION | 6 |

| 01 | TOOLS OF THE TRADE | 10 |

Your kitchen 12
Correct oven and hob use 13
Chopping boards and knives 14
Equipment you'll need 15
Parchment and papers 18
Why you should buy a stand mixer 19
Basins, tins and dishes 20
Pots and pans 21

| 02 | THE BASIC INGREDIENTS AND TECHNIQUES | 22 |

Types of flour 24
Types of sugar 26
A word about fats 27
Yeast, starters and culture 28
How to make a sourdough starter 29
Tips on making bread 30
How to make bread 32
The rise of real bread 34
Creaming together and the all-in-one method 35
How to make cake 37
Greasing and lining tins 38
Tips on making pastry 41
How to roll out pastry properly 43
How to make shortcrust pastry 44
How to make choux pastry 46
How to make suet pastry 48
How to make puff pastry 49
How to make flaky pastry 50
How to make meringues 52
How to make buttercream 54
How to make jelly 55
How to whip cream 56
How to make proper custard 57
Working with chocolate 58

| 03 | SAVOURY THINGS | 60 |

Easy white loaf 62
Brown loaf 63
Sourdough loaf 65
Ciabatta 66
Focaccia 68
Fougasse 69
Soda bread 70
Rye bread 71
Brioche burger buns 72
Flat breads and chapatis 73
Crumpets 74
Fool's gold loaf 75
Pizza 76
Pissaladiere 78
Sausage rolls 79
Meat pies 81

| 04 | SWEET BREADS AND LARGE CAKES | 82 |

Victoria sponge 84
Banana bread 86
Scones 87
Tea bread 88
Coffee and walnut cake 89
Christmas cake 90
Icing on the cake 91
Dorset apple cake 92
Lemon drizzle cake 93
Parkin 95
Chocolate cake 96
Orange and saffron cake 97
Pear upside down cake 98
Beetroot cake 99
Carrot cake 100

05 BISCUITS, SWEETS, BUNS AND SMALL CAKES   102

Shortbread	104
Millionaire's shortbread	105
Hot-cross or not crossed buns	106
Fat rascals	107
Gingerbread	109
Chelsea buns	110
Buns of Britain	112
Flapjacks	113
Home-made hobnobs	114
Apple roses	117
Profiteroles	118
Chocolate eclairs	120
Chocolate chip cookies	121
Jammy dodgers	122
Rocky road	123
Fudge	124
Biscotti	125
Muffins	126
Brandy snaps	127
Brownies	128
Eccles cakes	129

06 PIES AND TARTS   130

Apple pie	131
Cherry pie	134
Treacle tart	135
Portuguese custard tarts	136
Mince pies	137
Chocolate tart	138
Tarte tatin	139
Tarte au citron	140
Gypsy tart	142
Key lime pie	143
Fruit tart	144
Pecan pie	145
Baked cheese cake	146
Lemon meringue	147
Fig tart	148
Pumpkin pie	149

07 BAKED AND STEAMED PUDDINGS   150

Apple crumble	152
Apple strudel	153
Bread and butter pudding	154
Syrup sponge pudding	155
Sticky toffee pudding	157
Queen of puddings	158
Cherry batter puddings	159
Bakewell pudding	160
Rice pudding	162
Cambridge burnt cream	163
Hollygog	164
Swiss roll	165
Jam roly poly	166
Eve's pudding	167
Apple and rhubarb cobbler	168
Chocolate soufflé	169
Baked Alaska	170
Three Chimneys hot marmalade pudding	172
Lemon delicious pudding	174
Clootie dumpling	175
Pavlova	176
The history of Eton Mess	177

TROUBLESHOOTING   180

INDEX   182

INTRODUCTION

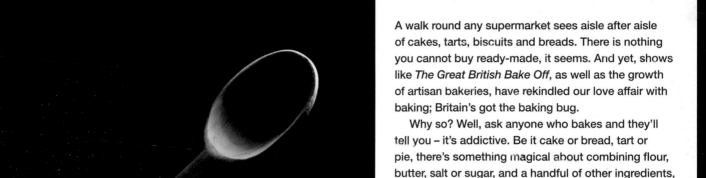

A walk round any supermarket sees aisle after aisle of cakes, tarts, biscuits and breads. There is nothing you cannot buy ready-made, it seems. And yet, shows like *The Great British Bake Off*, as well as the growth of artisan bakeries, have rekindled our love affair with baking; Britain's got the baking bug.

Why so? Well, ask anyone who bakes and they'll tell you – it's addictive. Be it cake or bread, tart or pie, there's something magical about combining flour, butter, salt or sugar, and a handful of other ingredients, and getting something warm, fresh and delicious out at the end.

Also, baking forces you to share your efforts. No one sets out to make two hot cross buns, or a single slice of tart: this is food for sharing with friends and family. A loaf or cake fresh out of the oven triggers something primal in us humans – it's a smell we respond to. What sort of person says no to a slice of something home-made? A person with a cold heart, that's who.

What you'll find in the pages of this book, then, are recipes for the classics; breads, cakes and puddings that have stood the test of time. Because I believe it's only when you've got your head around these that you can start to tweak, to adapt, and to customise.

WE NEED TO TALK ABOUT BREAD

How the UK ended up with some of the worst bread in Europe is a tragedy we're only just waking up to. Bread, the staff of life, was once so precious to our survival that barely a crumb was wasted. Now, one slice in three of a commercially made loaf goes in the bin. Of all the food we buy, bread suffers the most. That's wasteful.

Around 80% of the bread we eat in the UK is made by mega bakers using the Chorleywood breadmaking process – you can read more about this on page 34. Most of the remaining bread is produced by in-store bakeries, with local, traditional bakers making up the last few per cent. That's the wrong way round.

Making bread is easy. All you need is flour, water, yeast, salt and the time to smash them all together. Once you've mastered a basic dough, you can play around with its size and shape, and begin to explore adding extra flavours and enriching the dough.

CAKES AND PUDDINGS

No meal would be complete without the final course – pudding. Sweet in taste, yes, but not just for the sake of it. A good pud shouldn't be nothing but sugar, there should be depth and flavour too. It should have other flavours to harmonise its sweetness; the sharpness of a Bramley apple, the bitterness of chocolate, and the creaminess of, er, cream.

Then there's the matter of texture, from the solidness of a tea bread to the wobble of a baked custard. Finally, while nearly all of the ingredients in your main course are the same temperature, puddings let you have a contrast ranging from cool to just-out-of-the-oven hot.

We now eat dishes from all over the world – Mexican on Monday, Chinese on Tuesday, Indian on Wednesday; yet I bet you'd be hard pushed to name five puddings from any of those cuisines. And since it's a strange cook that would serve spotted dick and custard after pad Thai, many cooks don't bother with pudding. Add to this people's concerns about sugar levels and tooth decay and the upshot is – people are skipping pud.

And that's a shame. Pudding doesn't have to be a huge slab of stodgy sponge and custard you could grout a bathroom with. It can be a slice of something warming, home-made and – yes – good for you.

This book, then, is all of the above put into practice. These are real family-favourite puds, cakes and breads, the kind us British are famous for. While there's a few foreign stars – tart citron, key lime pie – there's also the kind of puddings your grandmother probably used to make. Just remember to leave a bit of room after your main course.

WHAT EXACTLY IS PUDDING?

With typical British confusion (think 'tea' the drink and 'tea' the meal) pudding is both the name for the course, and also a type of food served during it. What's more, puddings can be savoury – black pudding, steak and kidney pudding – as well as sweet.

'Dessert' is the American term for pudding. In the UK dessert traditionally meant an extra course *after* pudding, when the table was cleared, the cloth removed and a selection of fruit and nuts was presented along with sherry, Madeira or other fortified wine. Sweet is another term, now considered *déclassé,* and is to be found in John Betjeman's excellent poem 'How to get on in society'. Calling it 'afters' is just plain weird.

So, the course is called pudding, even if you've just finished eating a pudding and are serving something sweet – got it?

PERFECT PASTRY

Between bread and puddings lies pastry, happy to hold both sweet and savoury fillings, and equally as happy with a lid on as a pie, or open-topped as a tart. Being able to turn out an evenly blind-baked crumbly tart case is a skill well worth mastering. From there, a world of potential fillings opens up, allowing you to adapt to what's best and what's in season (usually the same thing). In the summer months, fresh fruits on cooling *crème pâtissière* is a must, while in the autumn and winter months apples and nuts are your friends.

There's a statistic somewhere that says that people cook less than 10%, often even less, of the recipes in the cookbooks they own. While I'm no completist either, if you're going to do anything from this manual, learn how to make good bread dough, a well-baked tart case and a classic sponge mix, because with these three skills you can do anything. Right, enough of the jibber jabber – let's kick off in the kitchen and talk kit.

CHAPTER 1
TOOLS OF THE TRADE

You don't need to spend loads of cash, but, unlike most cooking, baking does require you to get some basic kit before you get going. Most things you can buy budget versions of before upgrading later as money allows, but the thing I'd advise spending the most on from the get-go are your baking tins. These will hold your hard work in the oven, and if they're cheap and thin they'll distort in the oven or cause your cake mix to stick or cook unevenly, resulting in a poor bake. Also, beware the amazing window displays in kitchenware shops, and the lure of glowing reviews of seemingly amazing gadgets and gizmos online – you can easily end up buying things you probably don't need. Finally, if you look after your kit it should last for years.

Your kitchen

Your kitchen is your stage, your laboratory, your workshop – this is where the magic happens. There are some key things to think about when cooking in your kitchen. It's better to work in batches; do the preparatory work, then clear down and tidy up before starting the next stage. Making bread, cakes and puddings can have you moving between the hob, oven, fridge and even freezer, so you need to know where things are and work in an efficient and clean manner.

Needless to say, ovens cool when the door's left open for too long, and fridges rise in temperature. This can affect cooking time for things like cakes and setting time for things like jelly.

Workspace is critical – the bigger the better. Now, I know what you're thinking: 'How can I get a bigger kitchen?' But you don't have to move house, you just have to make the best use of the one you've got. Keeping surfaces free of jars and clutter leaves more room to work. This is especially true if you're rolling out pastry, for example. So move the kettle, tea caddy and bread bin and you'll reclaim the space. If your kitchen was designed by someone who hates food and has few work surfaces, consider working on the dining table.

Also, with pastry and bread work you'll often be flouring your work bench, so make sure you give it a good clean before starting. I prefer working directly on the worktop rather than on a chopping board. Not only are most chopping boards not big enough, but being made from wood and often full of grooves from chopping means that your dough often sticks to them.

When flouring your bench you only want the merest dusting – don't go chucking loads on, as eventually this will be incorporated into your dough or pastry and will increase the amount of flour in the recipe.

No matter what you're making in the kitchen, it's a lot easier to clean as you go. A sink piled with dishes and a counter splattered with food are no good to anyone. You're going to have to clean it up anyway so you might as well do so in small

bits rather than all at once. If the kitchen looks like a bomb's hit it every time you make a simple apple pie, you might want to have a word with yourself; that's not the best way to work.

Many chefs keep a jug of hot water on the side with spoons and forks in. It's these that they use repeatedly to taste their cooking. It also saves using either a clean spoon every time or your fingers – *don't* use your fingers. Tasting is important. It allows you to judge not only flavour, but also texture: is there the right amount of cinnamon in those stewed apples? How does that whipped cream feel in the mouth? These little details are what makes the difference.

Correct oven and hob use

Go into your kitchen and take a look at your oven in the cold light of day. Could it, perhaps, do with a clean? Has the bulb gone? Give it a bit of attention, because it's in here that the success of your baking efforts will literally rise or fall. Ovens are a once-a-decade purchase, if that – indeed, you're probably more likely to get a 'new' oven by splitting up or moving house than by buying a new one.

OVEN THERMOMETER

See that small knob on your oven the size of your thumb? Turning that changes your oven from room temp to around 230°C over just three-quarters of a turn. This makes most ovens very inaccurate at precise temperature measurement, which is critical for baking. It's far better to spend a few pounds on an oven thermometer which will tell you exactly how hot it is inside your oven. And if you've got a digital oven fan, you're still beholden to know where the thermostat is situated, which is normally towards the back. Point is, knowing what's going on where the action is is important. So is being able to see in, so give that see-through oven door a scrub too.

DON'T OPEN THAT DOOR!

Once your cake mix is in the oven, don't open the door until at least three-quarters of the baking time has elapsed. This is because the air bubbles coated in the butter, and held in place by the egg and gluten in the cake, are expanding due to the heat; eventually the cake will rise no more, and become fixed in shape. It's at this point you can sneak a peek. You also might want to turn the cake around. I do this as my oven sometimes runs a little hotter on the right-hand side, resulting in a slightly uneven colouring.

GLOVES

Get yourself a big, thick pair of oven gloves. I tend to favour two mitts, with a long sleeve, rather than those 'handcuffs' types, which are only good for lifting out casseroles. It's worth shelling out a few extra quid here, even if you've got asbestos hands. You don't want to drop your baking efforts because they're too hot, or struggle to get them into the oven. Me, I don't trust the silicone ones, and remain faithful to the fabric type.

Oven temperatures

A word about oven temperatures in this book. Nearly everyone these days has a fan-assisted oven measured in degrees Celsius, so all the cooking times are given for that. If you've not got a fan oven, up the temperature by about 20°C. If you've got a gas mark oven, there are conversion tables online.

Chopping boards and knives

CHOPPING BOARDS

How many chopping boards do you have? I've got nearly a dozen. I've big thick ones for heavy chopping, long flat ones with plenty of room, and small ones for slicing smaller things. You can never have too many in my opinion. They don't have to be expensive, but remember thinner ones made of plywood will warp over time, especially if they've come into prolonged contact with water. A piece of damp kitchen roll, or better still J-cloth, placed underneath whichever board you use will keep it from moving about.

KNIVES

Cooking starts, and in many ways, ends, with a knife, from peeling the first apple to slicing a wedge of the finished apple pie; so you

need a good blade in your hand. I'm constantly amazed at the state of Britain's knife drawers. Most people, I think it's fair to say, buy a knife and then never sharpen it again. Blunt knives require more pressure to use, meaning you're more likely to injure yourself. What's more, they don't cut but instead crush items apart, resulting in a messy finish.

Buy a good knife and look after it is my advice. Whilst a large 9in chef's knife is great for most kitchen tasks, for baking you'll also need a bread knife and paring knife. The former is good for slicing the heavier cakes and loaves, while the latter comes into its own when performing fruit preparatory tasks such as peeling and coring apples and hulling strawberries. They're also the best for trimming pastry due to their lightness.

KEEPING A KNIFE SHARP

A steel is a round bar with tiny grooves on that sharpens a knife by repeatedly running it up and down it at the correct angle. To be honest, unless you're a chef and use one every day they're probably not worth the money. Far better to invest in a whetstone and sharpen your knives once every few months on that. It doesn't look as showy and cheffy as using a steel, but you'll not have someone's eye out or loose a thumb, and it'll actually get your knives sharper. Other knife sharpeners require dragging the blade between two grinders; to be honest, I've had limited success with these, hence buying a proper whetstone. Having said all this I do have one friend who sharpens her knives on the upturned bottom of a mug!

Equipment you'll need

They say a bad workman blames his tools, but it's a terrible workman who attempts a job without *any* tools. You can't make, cook and serve cakes, buns, bread, tarts or puddings without some basic tools. But more than that, if you're offering people a portion of apple crumble off a fish slice, or peeling apples with a bread knife, you're going to look silly or, worse, injure yourself. This is a list of the equipment found in my kitchen drawer.

SPOONS

Now, chances are you've probably got teaspoons and dessert spoons in your cutlery drawer, but you should also invest in some nice big serving spoons. These are useful not only in making puddings, but in serving them too. You can't serve a decent man-sized portion of apple crumble with a dessert spoon, you'll just make a mess.

SPATULAS

These flexible friends are essential for smoothing out cake batter, as well as scooping up whipped cream or meringue from the bowl. Plastic ones are best as they'll not 'puncture' the cake mix by cutting harshly through it. They're also bendy.

PALATE KNIFE

An item it's nice to have in your drawer. Its large, round, thin metal blade is adept at lifting biscuits and other items off hot baking trays, and it can also be used for smoothing out fillings or toppings.

PASTRY BRUSHES

You'll need one of these for glazing if you're attempting any sort of baking. In the past most were made from hair, and later, artificial fibres, but today they're mainly made from silicone rubber. While this makes them easy to wash up and removes any chance of getting hair in your pud, they don't always have the bristle count to cover a pie sufficiently. In an emergency, use a *clean* paintbrush.

MEASURING SPOONS AND JUGS

It's harder than you think to judge amounts by eye, and most people overcompensate, so investing in a bunch of decent measuring spoons and a measuring jug is a good thing. There is much debate as to whether teaspoon measures of a substance should be heaped or levelled off. I favour slightly heaped. What does matter, though, is *not guessing*. As for jugs, I've found glass ones are good, but do look after them as in the past I've seen the numbers wear off over time in the dishwasher, leaving you with just a jug.

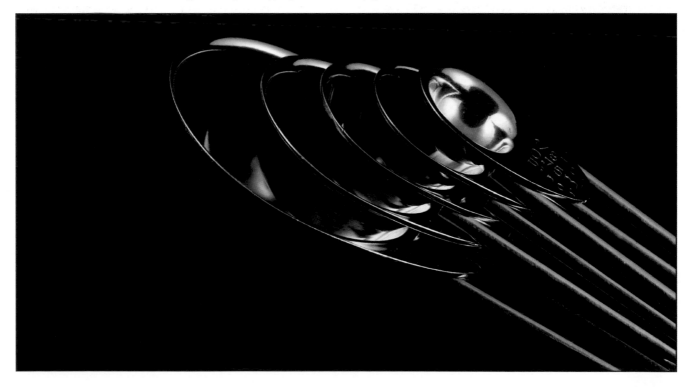

PEELERS

My mum and sister still peel apples and pears (and veg, come to think of it) with a small veg knife, saying they just can't get to grips with a peeler. I, on the other hand, swear by peelers. There are two main types. The traditional or Lancashire peeler has the blade in line with the handle and is the one your granny probably had. The 'modern' peeler is more like a disposable razor and has the pivoting edge held perpendicular to the handle – It's one of these you want to use.

TONGS

By no means essential to the making of most puddings, but a useful piece of kitchen kit to have, and if you're shopping for any of the other items on this page pick up a couple of pairs of these too.

WHISKS

Time was things like cream were whipped by hand in large bowls with big balloon whisks the size of a rounders bat, and getting four pints of cream to soft peaks is a lot harder than you think! I once interviewed Gary Rhodes, who told me a story about when he was visiting one of his restaurants in the Far East to see the chefs

cook his recipes. He saw one chef swirling his fingers in a bowl of cream. 'What are you doing?' he asked. 'Following the recipe, chef,' came the reply. 'That's not in the recipe!' Gary said. 'Yes it is,' replied the chef, 'here – it says "whip by hand!".'

Nowadays we're more likely to use an electric whisk or a stand mixer, but it's still worth having a small whisk in your kitchen drawer, however, as you'll sometimes want to mix things more gently than a machine can manage, as well as combining or melting things and making Italian or Swiss meringue. Like tongs, they're useful for savoury cooking tasks, like making a roux-based sauce.

TEA STRAINERS

Not just for a proper cuppa, these are also invaluable for getting little bits of things like seeds out of liquids and such, as well as dusting sugar or flour over the top of cakes and breads.

GRATERS

You've probably got a sort of triangular cheese grater. That's fine, but it's not the easiest thing to grate, say, nutmeg on without losing your fingertips. I suggest a micro planer, or just buy pre-grated nutmeg (it's better to grate your own, mind).

SCALES

If you're going to bake, you've got to weigh things out properly – 'guessing' the amount is just messing about. Consequently you need a good set of scales. Go digital is my advice as they're much more accurate. Digital doesn't have to mean expensive, however – you can pick up a set of scales for under a tenner. Get these first, and then if you find over time they're not big enough, or are starting to feel a little flimsy, you can then upgrade to a larger set.

BAKER'S DOUGH SCRAPER

Professional bakers often have large metal scrapers for working the dough. They're great when you're working on a steel work bench, but they'll soon knacker a standard plastic-coated chipboard kitchen counter. Better to buy a plastic one – they're available for a few quid and will make moving, shaping and cutting dough much easier. They're handy for other things too, like smoothing icing over cakes, and once I even plastered a wall with mine (didn't use it again for baking, however).

ROLLING PIN

The cooking cudgel, rolling pins are the baseball bats of the kitchen. The cheapest of the cheap are wooden with no moving parts, plastic ones are available too. Other designs have a central drum that revolves round two handles, or if you're really serious consider a marble or ceramic one. These, unlike wood, stay colder, and heat is the enemy of all dough and pastry work. Whichever you use, remember to dust it with a little flour before you start rolling. Finally If you're ever somewhere without your kit, you could be like my granny who used an old bottle. Putting it in the fridge is even better.

PLASTIC TUBS AND BOWLS

Cheap as chips, these are great workhorses in the kitchen and can be used for everything from marinating meat to proving dough. They're also great for storing fillings for tarts and pies, and soaking fruit for rich tea breads and such. Get down the pound shop and buy a job lot of varying sizes.

RULERS AND GUIDES

Here's a tip I adapted from my ceramics teacher at art school. If you're after a consistent thickness to your pastry and you've an ounce of DIY ability, make yourself two rolling guides sticks. These need to be flat, wide batons of wood, about the thickness of two pound coins on top of each other. Placing these either side of your pastry, and your rolling pin on top of them as you roll, ensures it ends up an even depth. You might be able to buy these, but they're dead easy to make from an off-cut strip of wood.

Alternatively you can buy rolling pin guide rings or bands. These are stiff rubber bands of varying thicknesses that you fit over each end of your rolling pin to ensure that any pastry is always of an equal thickness. If you're planning on doing a lot of pastry work I can't recommend them enough, and again, they're not very expensive.

FLOUR DUSTER

You'll need to dust your bench and surface regularly when making pies, and a flour duster makes that process a lot easier. Some work simply by shaking, others have a spring-loaded trigger, or you can make one from an old jam jar by simply punching a few holes in the lid with a knife or skewer. They're also handy for dusting sugar on to things.

PIE FUNNEL

A pie funnel, also known as a pie vent or a pie bird, helps prevent a soggy middle in large pies. Today they're often shaped like baby blackbirds, mouth open, presumably after the 'four and twenty' that were baked in a pie in the old nursery rhyme. They're best used if you're making a really deep dish fruit pie. Not essential, but it's worth picking one up if you're in the kitchenware shop.

COOKS' BLOWTORCH

These are great for browning things like the top of Cambridge burnt cream (page 163) or meringues. However, many of the ones you see in kitchen shops are cheap and little more than glorified ciggy lighters, and will run out of gas after a few ramekins. Ones from professional catering suppliers tend to be far too expensive, so get yourself down the DIY shop and buy a cheap plumbers' blowtorch. They might not be the best for plumbing, but they're more than adequate for browning your baking.

CAKE LEVELLER

This is a sort of hacksaw cum cheese wire attached to something resembling a coat hanger that you can use to cut a cake such as a Victoria sponge in half evenly. They're not expensive, and again, if you're serious about baking particularly large filled cakes, they're a good investment. Otherwise just use a bread knife, but take it slowly.

CAKE DECORATING

Slightly outside the remit of this book, but if you're thinking of getting into cake decorating and showier cakes for weddings, events and suchlike, a whole other world of kit awaits. You could start, however, with a silver board on which to display your cakes.

Parchment and papers

BAKING BEADS

These are little balls of clay that sit on top of your baking parchment to weigh it down. Of course, you can use large dried beans, which work just as well. Or even rice or lentils.

BAKING PARCHMENT

Sounds like something the Egyptians would have used, but parchment, like foolscap, is just an olde worde for paper. In fact it's rather a modern product. The paper is coated with silicone, which makes it totally non-stick. It's normally white, rather than brown like greaseproof. They *say* it removes the need for greasing cake tins, but I still apply a thin film of butter just to be on the safe side.

GREASEPROOF PAPER

Similar to baking parchment, but often brown rather than white. To be honest I use this and baking parchment interchangeably.

CAKE TIN LINERS

You can now buy paper cake and loaf tin liners in packs for a few pounds, if you're doing a lot of baking. These are much more handy than cutting out strips and circles to line your tins.

OTHER THINGS

You can even blind bake with cling film in the oven – I know, mad eh? Yet I've seen it done. Your oven can't be too hot, and you have to layer the cling film to four or five sheets. You'll still need baking beads. If you do it right, the cling film will contract slightly as it heats up.

PRICK WITH A FORK

There are plenty of people who just prick the whole base all over with a fork. All paper and beads do is keep the bottom of your pie or flan flat and stop it from browning too much. It all depends what your filling is, and how wet it is. A rule of thumb is the wetter and heavier the filling, the more you want to blind bake the base.

Why you should buy a stand mixer

Now, I'm a great believer in the idea that you don't need hundreds of pounds' worth of equipment to start baking, and I reckon that to buy most of the other items in this book that you'll need shouldn't cost you more than about £50.

However, while a handheld whisk is OK for whipping cream, it's not as versatile, stable or – let's face it – as cool as a stand mixer. If you're serious about baking, then investing in a stand mixer, a bowl and a whisk attachment is what you need to do. They cost a few hundred pounds, but they'll save time and will last a lifetime.

Me, I favour Kenwood's K-Mix range. It's a great kitchen workhorse and has never let me down. What's more, the powerful 500W motor and big five-litre bowl is plenty big enough. The main attachments are a dough hook or hooks for making breads, a creamer beater, a paddle beater for making sponge (which on a Kenwood is the iconic shape of a K), and a balloon whisk for whipping egg whites and cream. The K-Mix also has a variety of attachments for other cooking tasks, like grinding meat or rolling pasta.

So do you need a stand mixer? Yes, yes you do.

Basins, tins and dishes

I'd always recommend springform cake tins, as they make it much easier to remove your cake. In springforms the edge of the tin is held in place with a latch that pulls it flush with the bottom. At the very least go for a removable-bottom tin. The only time you don't need one is if you've two shallow sandwich tins, as cakes can come out of these quite easily.

Tins come in all sorts of shapes, depths and sizes, and yours might be totally different to mine. What's more, you can choose to make a cake round, square or oblong. Most of the recipes in this book are for 20cm cake tins unless specified, but do experiment with other sizes and shapes. Also, if you need to you can bake in anything – bread made in flower pots, cakes baked in cups (why do you think they're called cupcakes?) and so on.

Here's what I'd recommend as a good range of kit for the home baker. Add equipment piece by piece as you need it, rather than buying loads of stuff in one go. That way, you'll have time to get familiar with it. National treasure Mary Berry once told me she still bakes in the tins she got as a wedding present 'many years ago', admitting she'd be totally stumped if she had to use say a brand new silicone casing to make a cake.

- **Various-sized mixing bowls, both plastic and ceramic.** Big bowls are also great for proving bread in.
- **20cm springform tin.** Good all-round tin for cakes. The high sides mean the mix can rise but won't ever spill over.
- **20cm square loose-based tin.** These are best used for brownies and parkin.
- **2lb loaf tin (23cm x 13cm x 7cm).** Use these for not only baking bread, but also for fruit loaves.
- **25cm+ shallow flan tin with removable bottom.** These are best used for things like tarts.
- **25cm+ deep-sided flan tin.** Best for deep filled dishes like pecan pie and quiches.
- **4 crumpet rings and one large baking ring.**
- **1 muffin tray.** I favour the slightly shallow ones. You can also use this for making your Yorkshire puddings.
- **4 mini tartlet tins with removable bases.** Great for little showy tarts.
- **6 ramekins or *crème brûlée* dishes.** Essential for Cambridge burnt cream (page 163), but can also be used to serve things like olives.
- **Swiss roll tray.** Obviously a critical piece of kit for making Swiss rolls and roulade, but can moonlight as a standard baking tray as well.
- **Baking sheets.** A flat, non-stick baking sheet is essential for loaves, biscuits and cookies, basically anything made without using a tin. You want a range of sizes, from a 'width of your oven' big one to a few smaller ones. I think sheets with a very slight lip are best.
- **Bannetons.** These are wooden baskets made from a spiral of cane that give loaves that distinctive circular pattern on top. You can also prove bread in them. They're not essential, or that cheap (around £15), but they'll make your bread look more professional.

Another thing worth a look is a Lékué silicone bread maker. While we've had silicone bakeware for a few years now, this takes things a step further. It's a silicone bowl in which you can mix all the bread ingredients together and let it prove. You can then fold over one edge and hook it into the other side, making an oval shape, and transfer straight to the oven to bake. This saves on space and washing up – genius.

Pots and pans

Now, although this book is all about things you bake in the oven, some tart and pie fillings might need to be pre-made on the hob, so I thought I'd include a little about pots and pans. I think you only need non-stick for frying or sautéing – regular saucepans can be either. Generally non-stick pans are more delicate, and eventually, even if you never put a metal utensil near it, the non-stick coating does wear out. There's also been some health and environmental concerns about non-stick.

Here's what I think a basic kitchen should have:

Milk pan: a small pan that's great for doing things like warming up an apricot glaze or melting chocolate. I'd buy a few of these.

Medium saucepan: a mid-sized all-rounder pan. Try to find one with high sides – this helps keep things in if you're doing some frantic stirring of something like a flapjack mix. Best to have at least two or three of these in the kitchen also. Glass lids are best as you can see what's going on inside without taking the lid off.

Large saucepan: still may have a handle like its medium brother, but is a better pan for cooking bigger amounts of things like fruits.

Stockpot: as well as being for stock, you'll need a big pan like this for boiling puddings like clootie dumpling (page 175).

Steamers: perforated containers that sit on top of saucepans – these are good for cooking vegetables such as broccoli and other greens that you then might use in quiches. By steaming them to al dente, rather than boiling, they keep their shape and structure rather than turning to mush.

You also need a pizza stone, which is great for making pizzas with a really dry, crispy bottom, as well as other tin-less breads. Just don't ever wash it – water will soak into the porous stone and expand next time you use it in the oven, causing the stone to crack. If it gets dirty and has burnt bits on, scrape them off with a knife or even a wallpaper stripper.

Finally, although they're not really used in baking much, a good frying pan and a casserole are a must in any kitchen.

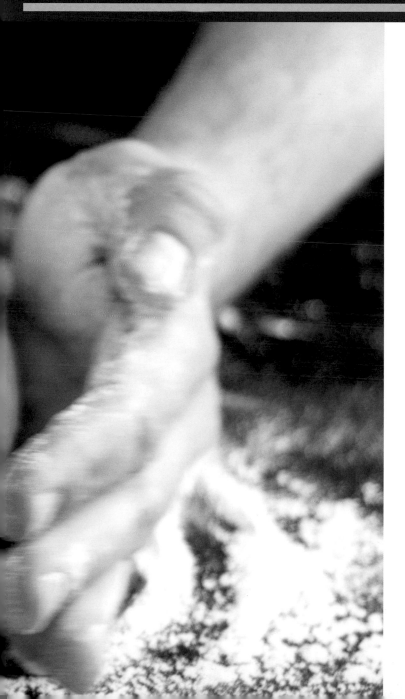

CHAPTER 2
THE BASIC INGREDIENTS AND TECHNIQUES

Baking is a combination of basic ingredients transformed using a few simple techniques. Doesn't sound that complicated, does it? Well, as ever, the devil is in the detail. What follows are the main techniques for making cake mix, bread dough and pastry. With these basic skills under your belt you can do a great many things.

Types of flour

There's not much baking that doesn't feature flour, so here are some of the main types and their uses. Also, there's no need to sift flour. This is a throwback to the time when poor-quality flour was bought from the grocer from a large communal barrel, into which anything might have fallen. You sieved it to get out flies, bugs and other 'extras'. All this talk of adding 'air' by sieving is, I think, nonsense. Having said that, if your flour's a little old and clumpy, breaking it up via a sieve is probably worth doing.

STORING FLOUR

It may seem inconsequential, but the flour you choose is important. This, after all, is going to make up a large part of the volume of your cake or pudding. Flour doesn't last forever. If you've had an old dusty bag kicking about in a cupboard for a year, chances are it's not going to be in peak condition for whipping up a stunning cake or pud.

Store flour in an airtight container in a cupboard in a cool part of your kitchen. Moisture and heat are the enemy of flour. Wholemeal flour doesn't keep as well as white flour as the oils from the wheat germ and bran can become rancid over time. Wholemeal flour will normally keep for about three months, while white flour keeps for around six. But given the cheapness of even premium range flours, it's worth buying fresh if you're planning something special. Whatever flour you choose, get to know it and see how it works in your baking, as different flours behave in different ways.

WHAT'S IN THOSE LITTLE GRAINS?

Each grain of wheat has three components: the bran, endosperm, and germ. Bran is the outer casing. It's sieved out of white flour, but you find it in wholemeal varieties. The endosperm is the white starchy body of the wheat. It's this that makes up the bulk of the flour. Finally, the germ is the reproductive centre of the grain, and contains nutrients and vitamins.

PLAIN FLOUR

Plain flour is milled wheat with the bran and germ removed. It's often bleached to give it a whiter appearance; unbleached versions are available but will be more creamy yellow in colour. If you're making pastry for a tart then shortcrust is what you should use.

SELF-RAISING FLOUR

Self-raising flour is just plain flour with baking powder added to it. Personally I think it better to use plain flour and just add your own baking powder, as that way you're in complete control. This, of course, means a little extra expense. A rule of thumb is to use four teaspoons of baking powder per 225g of flour.

STRONG OR BREAD FLOUR

Made from hard wheat, this has a higher gluten level and is mainly used to make various breads. However, it does have uses in pastry; hot water crust and flaky pastry use strong flour, as well as classic puff pastry. The British climate isn't ideal for growing hard varieties of wheat, so they're often imported from Canada, Europe and the USA.

WHOLEMEAL FLOUR

The whole kit and caboodle, this is flour with everything left in. Consequently wholemeal is incredibly good for you, but does give a more rustic look to pasty. You may need to up the liquid content when using it as it absorbs more water than white flour. Also the bran can inhibit the release of the gluten; you can compensate for this by adding a little white flour to your wholemeal bread – or vice versa, and make white bread a bit healthier by adding a bit of wholemeal.

GRANARY FLOUR

Sometimes called malthouse flour, this is a mix of wholemeal, white and a little rye or spelt flour as well as other malted grains to give a combined rustic style taste and texture. You can buy this ready mixed, or mix your own.

RYE FLOUR

Rye flour has less gluten than wheat flour, and consequently takes longer to rise. It's popular in Northern Europe in countries like Germany and Scandinavia. It has a lovely strong flavour, though, and can be used in combination with other flours.

SPELT FLOUR

An ancient variety of wheat that, like rye, has less gluten than wheat flour. It also has a nuttier flavour and again can be combined with other flours.

ORGANIC FLOURS

Many artisan bakers, particularly bread makers, favour organic flour. I have to say I've tried organic and non-organic and found no real difference between the two in my kitchen. However, organic flours nearly always tend to be stone-milled rather than roller-milled, and this traditional method leaves more of the nutrients intact, so there may be a benefit there. If organic's your thing, use organic flour. If not, don't.

GLUTEN-FREE FLOUR

Slightly outside the scope of this book but handy to know about in case you're ever baking for someone with coeliac disease. Your options are rice flour, cornmeal flour, potato flour or buckwheat.

OTHER FLOURS

Semolina is a very 'hard' flour produced from durum wheat. It's mainly used to make pasta. Cornflour, made from corn, or maize, is used in things like tortillas.

Types of sugar

There is a large range of sugars available in the shops these days, and they all have a use in baking in one form or another. If you're reading this outside the UK, note that, like flour, some sugars have different names in different parts of the world.

GRANULATED SUGAR

The classic sugar used for sweetening tea and coffee. You can also use this for baking when you've run out of caster sugar. The argument against is that because it's not as finely ground, it can give an ever so slightly gritty texture to your baking. But if you're just making a simple cake, or mucking about with the kids making biscuits, then you're fine.

CASTER SUGAR

Caster sugar is finer than granulated sugar, and consequently better for baking things like sponges or biscuits. Golden caster sugar is simply caster sugar that's not been refined as much – it has a subtle buttery, fudge-like flavour, so many people prefer using it. Plain white caster sugar is best used for things like meringues when you want to keep everything pure white.

ICING SUGAR

Icing sugar is simply granulated sugar ground down to a fine powder; an anti-caking agent is often added to stop lumps forming. Unsurprisingly, given its name, it's most commonly used for icing cakes. This is done by mixing the sugar with a small amount of water. It's also used in making buttercream for filling and covering cakes.

BROWN SUGAR

There's a variety of brown sugars and all of them can be used in baking and cake making. Essentially all brown sugars have a little more of the molasses remaining in them, giving them a more caramel-like flavour.

DEMERARA SUGAR

Demerara sugar is a light brown, large grain sugar and can be used to give a crunchy sweet texture. It's best used as a topping on biscuits, cookies, crumbles and such.

MUSCOVADO SUGAR

Comes in both light and dark varieties, the dark having more molasses remaining and consequently a stronger toffee-like flavour. Unlike demerara, muscovado isn't as free-flowing and is much more moist. It's best used in rich, moist, sticky things like fruit cakes and brownies, and pairs well with dark chocolate.

MOLASSES SUGAR

The darkest sugar you can get, almost black with a strong, treacle-like flavour. This is best used in solid darker cakes and things like fudge.

A word about fats

BUTTER

Good butter has taste and texture – it isn't some uniform yellow substance akin to Play-Doh. Much of baking is nothing without butter; from light-as-a-feather sponge cakes to flaky croissants, butter is the key. Fat, either butter or oil, is added to bread to make it softer and to contribute some flavour.

Most recipes call for unsalted butter but then add salt to the pastry or dough anyway. There's a reason for this. Firstly it lets you control the salt levels exactly – different manufacturers salt their butter at different levels. On the flip side, salted butter lasts longer in the fridge. Me? I use unsalted, but if salted is all I've got in the house and the shops are shut, who's to know?

Butter should be at room temperature (ideally 21°C) for making cakes. Too hard and it won't mix and incorporate; the same goes if it's too soft. For pastry cases for tarts and flans there's a rival technique you can try which calls for freezing your butter then grating into the bowl. I've tried it and it does work.

Always weigh your fat exactly. Too much will make the dough very short, meaning it'll be crumbly and difficult to handle. Too little and your pastry will be tough and dry. For cakes, too little and it won't be able to absorb the sugar flour and incorporate the air. The result will be a flat, solid cake.

LARD

You've got to feel a bit sorry for lard – it has none of the rural healthy glow of butter, no flowers are named after it, and its name is used in insults. And yet you bake pastry with half lard and half butter, and if offered an all-butter pastry most people will prefer the taste of the half and half one. Why? Well, because lard gives a different texture and taste to butter; they're like a fatty yin and yang, they complement yet contrast.

Lard's fall from grace was brought about by health concerns, despite the fact that lard has less saturated fat, more unsaturated fat and less cholesterol than an equal amount of butter by weight. Also, many commercial pie-makers avoid lard for cultural reasons. But trust me, it'll make your pastry 'short' and flaky and taste brilliant. Though mainly used in making pastry, there are some cakes that feature lard, most notably the aptly named lardy cake.

OIL

Most bread recipes use oil rather than butter, or a combination of the two. Obviously, for the more Latin breads, like focaccia and fougasse, you want to use olive oil. But vegetable oil is way cheaper than olive oil and much better for frying due to its higher smoking point. In fact most experts say you shouldn't fry anything in olive oil, and especially extra virgin olive oil – that's like cleaning your drains with champagne. I tend to use veg oil for most things, then buy a really good bottle of olive oil for dressings and for baking breads. Budget olive oil is the worst of both worlds.

Yeast, starters and culture

To make cakes or bread rise, you need a raising agent. These days we tend to use either baking powder or yeast.

WHAT IS BICARBONATE OF SODA?

Bicarbonate of soda is an alkaline powder that needs another acidic substance to react with, typically buttermilk or gone-off milk. (I once met a baker who swore gone-off milk and bicarb made the best scones!)

WHAT IS BAKING POWDER?

Baking powder is made from bicarbonate of soda (an alkali) to which cream of tartar (an acid) is added, as well as a filler – often cornflour or some other substance which absorbs moisture and stops it caking together. The acid and alkali react only when liquid is added, and produce carbon dioxide, causing the cake mixture to expand. This is why you should always add baking powder at the very last moment to any cake mix, and get your cake mixture into the oven immediately. A good rule is three teaspoons to 225g of plain flour.

WHAT IS YEAST?

To make bread rise, you need yeast. However, before the invention of baking powder in the 19th century yeast was used to raise many cakes too, though beaten eggs can also be used to help raise cakes.

Yeast is a single-cell organism that, as it grows, converts sugars and starches to carbon dioxide and a small amount of alcohol. It's the former of these two substances that causes breads to rise by expanding in a hot oven; the latter you can sometimes detect in a really good sourdough – it'll have an almost beer-like smell (it's not alcoholic, mind). In the past beer and bread making were much more closely linked, and beer once went by the nickname 'liquid bread'. Consequently there are two main types of yeast: brewer's yeast, and baker's yeast. The former is used for making beer and wine, and the latter for bread and cakes.

FRESH OR DRIED

For ease of use, dried yeast is much better. It gives good results and keeps for ages. Fresh yeast you'll sometimes see in health food shops or good real bread bakeries (they're more likely to have sourdough starters too). Fresh yeast lasts nowhere near as long as dried – a few days in the fridge at most. However, you can freeze it for three months. Also, you'll need to use around twice as much of it than you would dried yeast in any given recipe.

There's actually two types of dried yeast: original, and one called 'quick', 'instant' or 'fast-acting'. Original yeast needs to be brought up to speed by first mixing with a little warm water and sugar and leaving to develop for 15 minutes. Fast or instant yeast you can just add straight away.

STORAGE

Keep dried yeast in the fridge, tightly sealed, and let it warm up a little before activating. Also, pay attention to the use-by date, as after this the rising quality will begin to deteriorate and you may not get the desired results.

How to make a sourdough starter

An alternative to commercially produced dried yeast is to make your own starter. You may be surprised to know that there are yeasts all around us in the air, in the flour, on our hands. It's these that you can develop into a starter for baking. Historically all bread was made this way, and the 'mother', as starters were once called, was well guarded by bakers. After all, if it died or got damaged they'd be unable to bake.

You can make a sourdough starter in anything; at 'The Cake and Bake' show in 2014 artisan baker Duncan Glendinning and myself made a starter in a cement mixer and gave a cup each to every member of the audience.

Starting your starter, as it were, is easy. Begin with equal amounts of organic wholemeal flour and tepid water, mix together and leave in a warmish place. You don't want it in the fridge at this point, but exposed to the air and wild yeasts of your house. Feed and water it regularly, and in just over a week you'll have a starter that should be ready for baking with. Before you do give it a good feed to get it really going. When working, starters like to be between 22–25°C.

So, making it is fairly easy. Looking after it, however, is another thing. Remember, a starter is for life, not just for Christmas, don't let it die of neglect. You can become quite attached to your starters, letting the kids feed it daily at breakfast time, giving it a name, even taking it on weekends away. In one hip deli in Stockholm, Sweden, there's even a sourdough starter hotel where your starter can be looked after while you're away.

Before you start to make your starter, you need to think a little about the container it's going to live in. Many people favour sprung-top Kilner-style jars because they look retro, but actually most are too small. To be honest, you can keep one in a plastic tub with a lid. Whatever you use just remember it's got to have lots of room to add a couple of good spoons of flour in.

INITIAL QUANTITY
100g of stone-ground wholemeal flour
100ml of tepid water

FEED AMOUNTS
50g any flour
50ml tepid water

Place 200ml of tepid water in a tub and sieve in the flour. Stir gently with your fingertips (don't wash them prior to doing this, unless you've been to the bathroom!) and leave uncovered in a warmish place, no hotter than 25°C.

Feed it 50ml of water and 50g of flour each day. After eight or nine days it'll look bubbly and will have developed a telltale sour smell. This is a good thing.

On the tenth day it's ready to use. To get it revved up ('refreshed', as bakers say) discard half the mixture (or pour into another tub and give to a friend) and give it one more feed. Leave for six to eight hours, and then it's ready to bake with. See the recipe on page 65.

STORING YOUR STARTER
After day ten you should keep your starter in the fridge, where it will go to sleep. If you leave it any longer than two weeks it'll die. Remember to feed it once or twice a week. When you want to use it, take it out of the fridge six hours before you want to start baking and refresh it with a feed. So, for example, if you want to make bread on Saturday morning take it out before you go to bed on Friday night and give it a scoff.

Tips on making bread

At first making bread can seem a little daunting, and since you can now buy really good bread not from supermarkets but from the artisan bakeries that seem to be springing up in every city and town, why would you make your own? Well gents, it's a pride thing; and more than that, making your own bread – even if you don't do it every week – gives you an understanding of the relationship between wheat, water, salt, yeast and how they're all transformed by the power of heat. Practice makes, if not perfect, then at least progress with bread.

Furthermore, bread's something you can eat for breakfast, lunch and dinner, unlike cake. Finally, the smell of freshly baked bread triggers something in our brains, an ancient memory perhaps, something primitive and simple and good. The smells of fresh coffee, curry or cake are good, but bread beats them all by a nose.

Measure all the ingredients, particularly the salt, rather than just throwing in a pinch, as it's critical for flavour. If you've ever been on holiday to Tuscany you'll know they eat *pane toscano*, which is bread made without any salt that's strangely bland in the mouth. The reason they do this is that it's often eaten with salty toppings like meat or cheese, and the combination would prove too overpowering.

When proving bread, place it somewhere warm, but not too warm. Places like airing cupboards and on top of radiators are often too hot. Just boil the kettle and place it near that in a warm kitchen. I wouldn't recommend ovens either, even on the lowest setting. This is because most ovens are fan-assisted these days, and the constant stream of air can cause the top of the rising to dry out. Another technique I've seen used is to pour a kettle of hot water over a clean tea towel, wring it out, and place that over the bowl. This provides heat and dampness, which yeast loves.

Breads like a very, very hot oven, so always cook on full whack, as-hot-as-it'll-go, maximum warp. They also like a steamy oven rather than a dry one. While the oven's preheating, place a metal tray in the bottom. After you've placed your bread in, throw a little water on to the tray and quickly shut the door. It'll produce a large cloud of steam that your loaf will love. Steam is critical for developing that telltale firm, chewy crust. Another option is to buy an empty water sprayer from a DIY shop or garden centre.

Bake your bread as high up in the oven as you can, as this will be the hottest area, even if you've got a fan oven. Remember, though, that it will rise up, so make sure you leave enough headroom.

DON'T BAKE YOUR BREAD FOR TOO LONG

You want to take your gently proving loaf and shock it in a hot oven; this will cause the water in the loaf to turn to steam, which helps raise it as well as keep it moist. Too long in an oven and it'll exhaust all the water, resulting in a hard, dry texture. Most small buns and breads need no longer than 20 minutes, and large loaves not much more than 30. If your bread is in longer than that you'll have a brick.

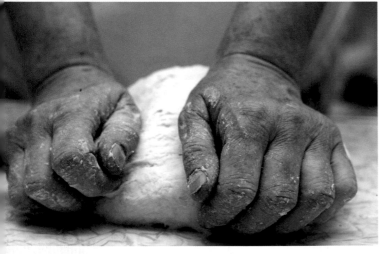

How to make bread

Measure the flour out into a bowl. If using butter, rub it into the flour so that it's dispersed.

Always add your salt and yeast well away from each other on opposite sides of the mixing bowl, rather than tipping one on top of the other. This is because if left in contact long enough the salt can kill the yeast, resulting in a flat, lifeless loaf.

Add your liquid, be it water or milk, and oil if using instead of butter, and begin to gently mix, with your fingers in a claw shape.

When you first start to work bread dough it can feel incredibly sticky, hence the temptation to add more flour. However, just keep working it, and as you build up the gluten it will hang together better and not stick to the surface as much. You're not kneading at this stage, just combining.

Once all the flour has been combined turn out on to your work surface and begin kneading the dough. This is essential to build up the gluten that will make the dough stretchier and eventually make it smoother. You should start to notice a shine developing on the surface of the dough.

Kneading takes longer than you think – at least ten minutes of hard pushing and pulling. You should get a bit of a sweat on!

Using your baker's scraper, keep the dough moving round. It should develop a 'top' that's less sticky than the 'bottom'. It's ready when it springs back after you prod it with your finger.

First prove. Dust your empty mixing bowl with flour or a little oil and place the dough with the 'top' face-down in the bowl. Note how big it is. Cover with cling film or a tea towel so a skin doesn't develop and leave somewhere warm to prove for an hour until doubled in size.

Knocking back. Using your fist or the heel of your hand, knock the air out of the dough. This helps build strength and texture in the bread. Transfer back to the bench and knead a little more, then smooth your bread into the desired shape.

Second prove. Place your loaf on a tray, or in a loaf tin if using, and cover again with cling film or place in a large plastic bag for 30 minutes or until the dough rises to the lip of the tin. Preheat the oven to at least 200°C.

Place the loaf in the oven and splash in some water to create steam. This is to help form a good crust.

Bake for around 25–35 minutes depending on the size and shape of your bread. Tap the bottom, and if it feels a little soft and leaden give it a bit longer – you're after a hollow sound. Leave to completely cool on a wire rack.

The rise of real bread

WHAT IS REAL BREAD?

Good question. The fact you're asking it shows that attitudes are beginning to change. The Real Bread Campaign exists to defend and promote traditional methods of making bread, and it defines real bread as being made from flour, water, yeast (either commercial or a natural sourdough starter) and salt. That's it. Anything else, and it's not real bread. These four ingredients have featured in bread, all over the world, since the rise of agriculture over 10,000 years ago. As their website says, 'If you add anything but salt to butter, you can't call it butter; if you add anything at all to milk, it's no longer milk. So why are we not afforded such legal protection when it comes to our daily bread?'

THE CHORLEYWOOD BREAD PROCESS

So, what's wrong with bread today? Well, if the story of bread has a villain, it's surely the Chorleywood bread process. I'm sure the initial intentions were good; post-war scarcity, hungry mouths to feed, and a broken and shattered nation. And so scientists at Chorleywood Flour Milling and Bakery Research Association laboratories began to look at how to make a loaf of bread quicker. By adding hard fats, twice as much yeast, and mixing using high-powered mixers before proving the resulting 'dough' in a vacuum, they came up with a process that reduced the time it took to make bread from a day to just over three hours, and a good chunk of that time was letting the resulting 'loaf' cool down enough so it could be put in a plastic bag. Crucially the technique allowed British wheat – which wasn't as 'hard' as American or Canadian wheat – to be used to make bread, meaning less reliance on expensive imports being shipped in.

The result? A soft, squishy uniform pre-sliced loaf that lasts for ages and is as cheap as chips. It also happens to have very little taste, texture or flavour and is full of lots of things that aren't flour, water, yeast or salt. Today, CBP-made bread accounts for nearly 80% of all bread sales in the UK. But worse, according to DEFRA 32% of bread purchased by UK households is thrown away when it could be eaten. In 2012 the anti-food-waste group WRAP said that 680,000 tonnes of 'avoidable' bakery waste is thrown away each year at a cost of £1.1bn, with about 80% of it from packs that have been opened but not finished. So not only is most bread rubbish, most bread goes on to become rubbish. It's madness.

A LITTLE TEST

Next time you buy (or make!) some proper bread do this little test. Take a slice of real bread, and a slice of supermarket bread, and squeeze them in your hands for 30 seconds. Let go, and the real bread should spring back. The ordinary bread stays tightly squashed. It has none of the strength of real bread.

Also, have you noticed how supermarket bread goes mouldy, rather than stale? Stale bread can still be put to good use in the kitchen – bread and butter pudding (page 154), or to make breadcrumbs for treacle tart (page 135); mouldy bread can only be put in the bin.

Creaming together and the all-in-one method

It sounds simple doesn't it, mixing ingredients together? But there's a knack to making cake mix that takes your efforts from ordinary to excellent.

CREAMING BUTTER AND SUGAR METHOD

Here comes the science bit. By creaming, you're breaking down the butter and incorporating the sugar as well as introducing tiny pockets of air to the mix. This will increase the volume and help your cake to rise. You're also softening the mixture, and it should turn a lighter colour than the bright yellow of pure butter due to the introduction of the air bubbles, which are now surrounded by the fat. When placed in an oven this would just melt and release the air, but thanks to the introduction of egg into the mix this doesn't happen, as the egg – particularly the egg white – surrounds and binds the structure in place.

Your butter must be at room temperature, or, to be more exact, 21°C. If it's too cold it's not pliable enough to incorporate air. Likewise if it's too warm it begins to turn liquid and, again, can't hold the air in place.

Cut the butter up into cubes about an inch square, and add to a deep bowl. Pour over the sugar and then place the whisk in and turn on slowly. You could even get things started with a spoon and mash the sugar into the butter a bit to stop it flying out when the spinning whisk hits it.

The old-fashioned way was to do this with the back of a wooden spoon like my gran did. The downside is it takes ages. These days it's much easier to use either a hand-held whisk or, even better, a stand mixer fitted with a paddle. Personally I wouldn't recommend a food processor, as the blades cut through the mix rather than beating air into it, unless it has a special 'whisk' tool.

THE ALL-IN-ONE METHOD

There are two schools of thought for making cakes, those that cream the butter and sugar together first as above, before adding the other ingredients like flour, eggs, baking powder and such; and those that favour the all-in-one method. As you'd expect, this requires you to place all the ingredients in a bowl at the same time and then mix.

Purists say you should do the former for a properly made cake; others more concerned with saving time favour the latter. In my opinion, creaming lets you control things more precisely, and is great if you've got the time. All-in-one is quicker and still gives good results.

How to make cake

Making sure that not only your butter but also everything else – milk, eggs, fruit – is at room temperature helps when making cakes. Talking of eggs, all the recipes in this book use medium-sized eggs, which according to the British Egg Information Service typically weigh between 53–63g. Always use free-range eggs; it's what the chicken would have wanted.

Always combine dry ingredients together first, before adding any wet ones.

Don't overfill the cake tin – you want the cake mix no more than halfway to two-thirds of the way up the side of the tin. Any more than that and your cake may spill over.

Unlike bread, cakes are best cooked in the middle of the oven. If you're baking two large individual sponges, try and fit them both on the same shelf. You can swap their positions once the cake has set. As mentioned in Chapter 1 (page 13), don't open the door for at least the first 20 minutes after the cake has gone in. Then, once it's fixed, you can turn it around.

If you put the cake on the top shelf, or if your oven is too hot, a crust forms on the top before the cake has finished rising; this crust then cracks as the cake pushes up from underneath it.

MIXING

Be sure not to *over*-blend your cake mix – this can lead to a flattened cake and a tight crumb with little air in it. It's time to stop when the mixture is light and creamy.

Always begin mixing on a slow setting; this will keep your ingredients in the bowl and not all over the work surface. As the mixture begins to become incorporated you can increase the speed a little.

Be careful when adding eggs. It's important to add them one at a time and wait until each one has been fully mixed in. If you add them all together your mix can curdle.

A spatula is a handy piece of kit here, to scrape down any mix that rises up the side of the bowl.

You can then add any other flavourings or ingredients the recipe calls for and gently combine together.

Greasing and lining tins

'Grease and line a baking tin' – you'll see this a lot in this book, and it sounds simple enough; but what does it actually mean, and why do it? Well, the simple reason is that lining a tin with parchment in combination with a fat such as butter or oil stops your cake from sticking to the sides of the tin.

Measure your parchment, cut and 'try out for size' before greasing your tin. Then, once you know it's the right size and shape, grease the tin before applying the paper. This will help it stick when you put it inside.

You only want a very small amount of grease. My old home economics teacher used to use the wrapper the butter came in. If you can see yellow bits of butter, you've probably used a bit too much. Other people melt the butter first, and apply with a pastry brush. You can also use vegetable oil sprays.

Place the parchment in the tin and run your fingers over to ensure a snug fit. I'd even recommend greasing and lining your tins if they're non-stick, just to be sure.

HOW TO LINE A ROUND TIN

On a chopping board, place the tin on a sheet of paper and hold in place with your hand or something heavy. Using a very sharp craft knife* or scalpel, cut around the tin; this should produce a perfect circle a tiny bit bigger than the inside of your tin. I prefer this over repeatedly folding the paper to make an arrow shape and 'guesstimating the centre of the tin' way, as I think it's more exact, especially on high-sided tins. Also, I don't like to use a pencil to draw around the tin and then cut out. You *can* do that, but I don't fancy graphite, however little, in my bakes!

* The other reason for having a craft knife, Stanley knife or scalpel in the kitchen is for scoring pork skin to make crackling. Be sure to wash it afterwards, mind.

HOW TO LINE A SQUARE TIN

Use the same process as a round tin: place the tin on a sheet of parchment on a large chopping board and cut around with a craft knife.

LINING THE SIDES OF A CAKE TIN

For most cakes you only need to line the bottom. If, however, you're cooking something like a fruit cake, which might be in the oven for a long time, line the sides.

To line the sides of a round tin cut two long strips 3cm bigger than the height of your cake tin. You'll need to overlap them inside the tin to ensure complete coverage. Alternatively you can unroll a lot of parchment and cut one long continuous strip, but that's a bit wasteful.

Using scissors, make lots of little snips about 0.5cm in length along one side of each piece; these will help the parchment bend. You should line the sides before lining the bottom of the tin. To line the sides of a square tin, use a ruler to measure the length of one side, multiply by four, add a bit for luck, divide by two and cut two strips to that length. Again, you want to line the sides first, before lining the bottom; and ensure there's a good fit, with about 3cm of paper standing above the lip of the cake tin.

HOW TO LINE A LOAF TIN

For loaf tins you want the parchment to extend up each end of the tin and over the side, so you can use it to help remove the cake from the tin. Cut a strip from the roll of paper as wide as your loaf tin – a 900g/2lb tin is normally around 7cm in width. Place in the tin before greasing to check the size is correct; you want two 3cm flaps hanging over the lip of the tin. If it looks OK, grease and line the tin.

TINS FOR BREAD

If you're baking bread in a loaf tin you don't want to use baking parchment. Instead, lightly grease the bottom and sides of the tin with a neutral oil such as sunflower or vegetable, then dust over a little flour. Shake this around to cover all the tin.

REMOVING THE CAKE FROM THE TIN

Once your cake is cooked, let it cool for around five minutes, and then remove. It will have shrunk slightly as it cools which should make it easier to get out of the tin. Don't go hacking at the edges with a palette knife – you'll just

scratch the tin's non-stick coating. Try using a spatula instead; but really, it should come out quite easily when you turn it upside down.

CAKE TIN LINERS

If all of the above seems like a faff, and money's no object, cake tin liners are available from cookware shops. Just make sure you get the right size for your tin.

Tips on making pastry

TEMPERATURE

According to an old wives' tale 'cold hands and warm heart' make the best pastry, and generally speaking the more you handle, prod, finger and move pastry, the more it gets annoyed and deteriorates. So it's best to handle it as little as possible. How you choose to combine your fat, flour and liquid is very important; these are the main methods.

FINGERTIPS

Using your fingers is by far the simplest way to mix pastry, and given that you probably already own a full set they're also the cheapest tool too. Mixing with your fingers allows you to judge the texture of your pastry as it's coming together. If it feels too wet you can add a little more flour; too dry and a drop more water is needed.

The downside with fingers is that they're warm, so if you spend too much time handling the mix you'll start to melt the fat. This is especially true for blokes like me with big, hot hands. Consequently you have to work quickly.

When using your fingers for rubbing in, always draw the flour and fat up out of the bowl to rub it, letting it fall back as it passes through your fingers.

A FOOD PROCESSOR

Food processors make mixing pastry easy, but you do have to be careful not to overdo it. The blade will produce some heat as it spins, so take it really slowly in gentle pulses rather than revving it at full whack.

THE TWO KNIVES METHOD

Favoured by my maternal Scottish grandmother, who made pie at least once a week in old enamelled tin dishes, this technique sees you incorporate the fat and flour using two knives, preferably round-ended butter knives. You make small cutting motions with the blades.

PASTRY BLENDER

An easier version of the two knives approach, some people swear by these. You use them like a potato masher. They break the fat up into tiny pieces that help produce a perfect flaky pastry.

RESTING PASTRY

Like bread dough, pastry needs plenty of rest in order to develop the gluten. Unlike dough, though, it likes a nice cool fridge rather than somewhere warm. This allows the fat to firm up again. Most pastry tips say roll the dough into a ball then wrap in cling film and put in the fridge. However, I prefer to use sandwich bags (they're reusable and sealable) rather than cling film. Also they have a white space on them where you can write what's inside, as well as the date – handy if you're going to freeze the pastry.

They're also easier to manage, as I don't know about you, but my roll of cling film *always* ends up out of the box and I'm forever picking along its length trying to find the edge. You only wrap it in plastic to stop it drying out.

Secondly consider the shape. If you put a ball of dough in the fridge the outside will get cold but the centre will probably still be warm after 20 minutes. So my advice is to squash the ball flat into a lozenge shape thereby increasing the surface area, which will let the cold penetrate deeper.

If you can rest pastry overnight it'll be even better. Finally, remember pastry freezes well, so always make more than you need. Then you'll have some ready to go for a midweek quick pie.

BLIND BAKING

You'll hear this term a lot in Chapter 6. It refers to pre-cooking the bottom and sides of a pastry case to ensure a good, firm bake and avoid the dreaded soggy and undercooked bottom. Often baking beads and greaseproof paper are used to weigh the pastry down during cooking (see page 18). Whichever method you use, make sure the pastry goes from a cold fridge to a hot waiting oven. It's that rapid temperature change that shocks pastry into action.

READY-MADE PASTRY

Sure pastry is easy to make, but sometimes you need to save time. That's where ready-made comes in. There are some really good all-butter ones on the market now; look out for these, and use any time you save to really go to town on the filling.

How to roll out pastry properly

COOL YOUR BENCH

Professional pastry chefs roll out their dough on a refrigerated block of marble, in a chilled room, at dawn. Here's the next best thing. Fill a baking tray with ice cubes and place on your worktop about ten minutes before you start working. This will chill it down. When you remove the tray check for any condensation. If there is any, wipe it away with kitchen roll. You want to begin on as cool and dry a surface as possible.

UNDER PRESSURE

Whatever rolling pin you've chosen (see page 16), how you roll is just as important. You want to apply gentle pressure, firmly, but don't force or chase the dough – you're not driving a steamroller. It's better to roll softer for longer.

ROLL FROM THE MIDDLE OUT

When rolling shortcrust pastry, start in the middle and roll upwards (away from you), then return to the middle and roll downwards (towards you).

MOVE THE PASTRY, NOT YOUR PIN

Don't come at your dough from crazy angles. Move and turn the dough gently, and keep your pin rolling straight ahead.

THE QUARTER TURN

As you roll you'll end up with two thicker ends; turning 45° flattens these down and ensures an even spread. Moving the pastry also helps stop it sticking to your work surface.

LINING THE TIN

You need to act swiftly when transferring your pastry to your baking tin. The best way is to gently loop the dough over your rolling pin and unfurl it like a magic carpet on to the waiting tin. You want to get this right first time, chaps, so place your tin over your pastry to see if it's big enough. Measure it, and try and imagine what you're going to do next.

Remember, it's not just the diameter of the tin you need to allow for – the pastry has to come up the sides and over the lip too. So you want it a good 2in to 3in bigger than your tin (depending on the deepness of it).

If you do misjudge it, you've got to work fast to get it rolled back loosely around you pin and try again.

ROLLING ON THE BASE PLATE

If you're using a large non-stick flan tin with a removable base you can also roll out your pastry on top of this – slowly, remember. Then, using a fish slice or a palette knife, lift the base and place into the outer ring and just work up the edges. This technique lets you get a very thin, flaky crust over a large area, and reduces the risk of it breaking. You'll still need to do quarter turns as you roll.

The fewer times you handle the pastry the better. Once your pastry is loosely over the tin, you need to work it into the corners. Jabbing at it with a hot pointy finger might poke through the pastry, or rip it, as well as not getting it flush into the tin. Instead take a lump of off-cut or leftover pastry, roll into a ball with your fingertips and pinch and hold at one end. You've just made a 'dabber'. Use the round ball end to gently press the pastry into the corner of the tin.

The dabber has another use too – it's your canary in the mine. I put mine on a baking tray with my pie. Though it's a different size, it allows me to judge how the pastry's behaving in the oven. If all is well you can even eat it as a cook's perk.

You can enrich your pastry by adding more fat and reducing the flour, or by adding eggs. However, this makes it a bit tricky to roll out and move about your bench. One answer is to roll out between two sheets of greaseproof paper. Remember, keep the pastry cool and the fat solid.

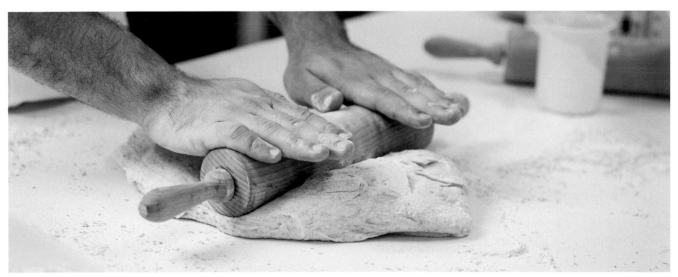

How to make shortcrust pastry

Rich and crumbly, sweet and golden, shortcrust pastry is, to my mind, an honest, homely sort of pastry. It doesn't get in the way of the filling, but supports it. It also happens to be the easiest pastry to make and in my experience the one that goes wrong the least often. I also happen to think it's the tastiest.

INGREDIENTS

- 400g of plain flour
- 100g of butter
- 100g of lard (or 200g of butter if you prefer)
- 30g of caster sugar
- Pinch of salt
- A few tablespoons of cold water

The rule of thumb for shortcrust is a ratio of around half fat to half flour. Unlike some other pastries you want your fat at room temperature for shortcrust. This is because it needs to be mixed with the flour quickly, and if it's too cold that will take longer.

If your bowl and fingers start to glisten, however, you've probably overworked the butter. I'd recommend stopping and putting it back in the fridge to cool things down a bit; you may need to add some more flour. Another danger is overworking the gluten in the flour by too much kneading. This will create a hard, tough pastry, rather than one that's light and flaky. Too much water is a bad thing too...

What you're after is a loose relationship between all these ingredients, where they're combined enough to hold together, but can easily yield to the slightest pressure from a fork when cooked. The French call this pastry *pâte brisée*.

When adding water to pastry, always make sure that it's as cold as possible. Let the tap run for a while, or put a small glass at the back of the fridge for 15 minutes before starting.

I've found that around 600g of shortcrust is more than enough for an open pie or tart in a shallow 23cm tart tin. Remember, the deeper your dish the more pastry you'll need.

It's far, far better to have pastry left over than to find yourself short. Butter and flour are not that expensive after all. Any leftovers or offcuts can be frozen, or used to make something else.

The procedure opposite is for sweet shortcrust pastry for puds; if you want to make a savoury pie using shortcrust pastry simply omit sugar from the ingredients.

Sieve the flour into a bowl and add the cut-up butter and lard.

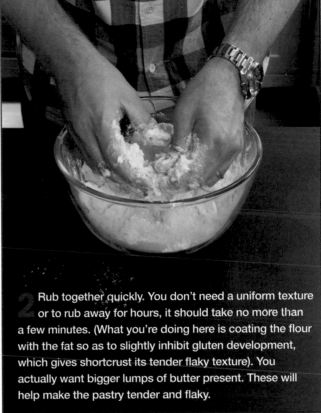

Rub together quickly. You don't need a uniform texture or to rub away for hours, it should take no more than a few minutes. (What you're doing here is coating the flour with the fat so as to slightly inhibit gluten development, which gives shortcrust its tender flaky texture). You actually want bigger lumps of butter present. These will help make the pastry tender and flaky.

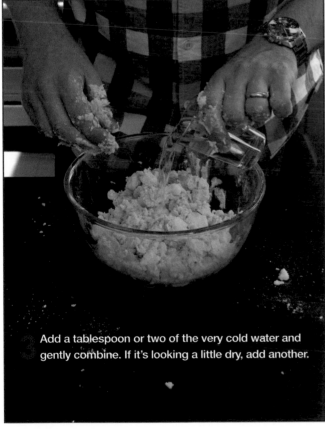

Add a tablespoon or two of the very cold water and gently combine. If it's looking a little dry, add another.

Bring together into a ball, squash it a little, and put in a sandwich bag in the fridge for at least an hour, two if you can spare it. It'll be quite happy in the fridge for 48 hours, however. When you come to need it, just roll out swiftly and transfer to your pie dish.

How to make choux pastry

Choux pastry is light, shiny, almost crispy pastry used in dishes like profiteroles and éclairs. Choux has a high water content, and it's the steam given off when the pastry hits the hot oven that enables it to rise and expand. Unlike other pastry, except perhaps hot water crust, choux is pre-cooked in a saucepan. Once cool enough to handle it's then piped on to a baking tray, either as small blobs for profiteroles or long fingers for éclairs. Needless to say, you'll need a piping bag to make them.

Once cooked it's important to cut a small hole in the base of each bun or éclair to let the steam out; if you don't do this it'll condense back into water as it cools, and your bake will be soggy. Of course, profiteroles and éclairs make use of this hole in the base by filling the centre with whipped cream. Choux pastry doesn't keep well at all, neither do the finished profiteroles or éclairs, so you want to make and bake it all in one go.

The following amounts will make about twenty 8cm éclairs, or thirty profiteroles:

INGREDIENTS

- 250ml water
- 100g unsalted butter
- 150g plain flour
- 3 eggs
- Teaspoon of salt and sugar

Savoury choux

You don't just have to stick to cream and chocolate for profiteroles and éclairs, you can make savoury versions too. Thin down some cream cheese with milk and pipe that in the centre, adding chives, garlic or pesto. Salmon pâté would work too, or what about blitzed mushrooms? You can even play with the presentation, scalping the top off each bun and filling the hole with savoury ingredients before popping the top back on at a jaunty angle.

Place the water, butter and sugar in a large pan and heat until the butter has all melted and the liquid comes to a rolling boil.

Turn off the heat and add the flour and salt all in one go. Place the saucepan on a tea towel to help keep it steady and with a wooden spoon beat together as hard as you can; as the mixture combines and gets thicker, increase the speed of your beating. When fully combined the mixture should come away from the sides of the pan.

Leave to cool for five minutes, then add the beaten egg bit by bit and combine until you have a stiffish, shiny mixture that drops off the spoon reluctantly.

When the dough is cool enough to handle, transfer to a piping bag. If you're making profiteroles you'll need a plain 1cm nozzle; for éclairs you'll need a 1.5cm fluted (the edge is zigzagged) nozzle. To fill your profiteroles or éclairs you'll also need a 0.5cm nozzle. All these should come with the piping bag if you buy it as a set. Alternatively, buy the nozzles and use disposable piping bags.

How to make suet pastry

Suet pastry is used in baked puds such as hollygog (page 164) and jam roly poly (page 166) as well as dishes like steak and kidney pudding.

INGREDIENTS

- 400g of self-raising flour
- 200g of beef suet
- Pinch of salt
- Around 150ml of water (enough to bring it together as a dough)

WHAT IS SUET?

Suet is the fat found around the internal organs of animals, mainly pork or beef in the UK. The best suet is found round the kidneys. It is a hard white crumbly fat, with a pleasant flavour and higher melting point than butter. Today it comes ready grated in packets, which makes it much easier to use (it must have been a nightmare using it in Victorian times), but some butchers still sell it fresh.

Vegetarian suet is made from palm oil combined with rice flour to resemble real suet, but it doesn't have anything like the flavour of real suet. However, this makes it a better choice for sweet puddings.

A rule of thumb for suet pastry is to use around half the weight of suet to flour.

1 Sieve the flour and the salt into a bowl.

2 Add the suet and combine thoroughly.

3 Make a well in the centre and add small amounts of water; slowly bring the dough together with a spoon until you can get your hands in.

4 It's ready when it's not too wet and no flour remains in the bowl. You might need to add a little extra water. Chill for 15 minutes before using.

How to make puff pastry

There are two critical ingredients in classic puff pastry: time and patience. Other than that it's virtually just butter, flour and water.

INGREDIENTS

- 150g of strong flour
- 150g of plain flour
- 140mm of cold water
- Juice of half a lemon
- Pinch of salt
- 300g of unsalted butter

It's not particularly hard to make, it's just very, very time-consuming; you've got to have time to make it, rest it, roll it, rest it, roll it and finally rest it some more. Only then is it ready to use. Even most chefs don't have time for that, so they buy it in.

Puff pastry gets its puffed-up appearance by rolling very thin layers of butter between layers of dough. As it cooks in a hot oven the butter melts, giving off steam and fat which causes the very thin layers of dough to puff up and colour. This gives a light, pleasing crunch in the mouth. The French call puff pastry *pâté feuilletée*, which means 'pastry made leaf-like'. Another name for it, and indeed for the pudding named after it, is *mille-feuille*, meaning 'a thousand leaves'.

METHOD

1 Mix together the flours, salt, juice of a lemon and water in a bowl. The dough will feel very dry and tight. Once it's come together, tip out on to the bench and knead for a good ten minutes. It will feel dry and gritty at the start, but keep working it to develop the gluten and eventually it will become smooth and firm.

2 Shape into a ball and cut a cross in the top (not all the way through) to make four petals. Seal in a plastic bag and put in the fridge for 2 hours, or even overnight.

3 When chilled, take out and open the four petals and roll each out to make a large cross.

4 Place your cold butter between two sheets of greaseproof paper and beat it to a flatness of about 1cm square.

5 Place the butter in the centre of the cross and fold the four petals back over it, squashing each down with your hand each time.

6 Put the pastry back in the fridge for two hours.

7 Take the pastry out of the fridge and roll into a rectangle about the length of a sheet of A4 paper but only two-thirds of the width.

8 You're now ready to 'turn' or 'book' the pastry. Fold the top third of the pastry into the centre, then fold the bottom third over that. Press together firmly, and stick your finger in it to make a single dent. Put it back in the fridge.

9 Repeat the 'turning' process three times, each time adding a dent so you know where you're up to. Once you've 'turned' it three times chill overnight again.

10 Take out and roll to the required size as fast as you can and get it into a blisteringly hot oven.

Told you it was time-consuming...

How to make flaky pastry

INGREDIENTS

- 220g of plain flour
- Pinch of salt
- 75g of lard
- 75g of butter
- 1 teaspoon of lemon juice
- Cold water

You'll know this pastry from such savoury favourites as sausage rolls. It doesn't puff up as much as classic puff pastry, and when it does it's in a much more random manner due to the dispersement of the blobs, but it does give you a good result without all the roll, chill, turn ad infinitum of classic puff.

Sieve the flour and salt into a bowl and rub in half the lard and half the butter. Add the lemon juice and enough cold water to bring together into a dough – around a few tablespoons should do it. In a separate bowl mix together the remaining butter and lard.

Roll the dough out into a rectangle around 25cm x 10cm.

Take a third of the fat mixture and place blobs of it on the top two thirds of the dough.

Fold the un-blobbed bottom third up over the middle, and carefully fold the top half down on to this. Gently squash together and chill for 20 minutes.

Roll out the dough again to 25cm x 10cm and repeat the previous stage using another third of the fat. Chill for 20 minutes, before doing it again with the final third of the fat mix. Chill again for 20 minutes or more.

When needed, roll out to the required size quickly and use as soon as possible.

How to make meringues

Meringue likes things clean; it likes your hands clean, your equipment clean, and your bowl clean. The slightest trace of grease (of which there is a lot in baking, given the amount of butter flying around the kitchen) and it strops off in a huff, refusing to play ball. Not only that, it hates moisture, prefers to be made in a glass or metal bowl, and likes a cooling, dry oven to cook in, preferably overnight. And finally, older eggs make the best meringues too. What a faff!

INGREDIENTS
- 150g egg whites
- 300g of caster sugar
- 2 teaspoons of cornflour (optional)
- 1 teaspoon of cider vinegar (optional)

These days there are two types of meringues: the traditional crispy kind, found in Eton mess, baked Alaska and pavlova, and the chewy kind, which have sort of become a pudding by themselves. These chewy versions see the addition of cornflour and white wine vinegar. Leave these ingredients out if you want a crisp meringue, and you'll also need to leave them in the oven a bit longer.

What's also become de rigueur is to add additional flavours to them, such as cinnamon or coca, or fruit colourings like raspberry. Or go all in and top with chestnut purée, caramelised nuts and dark chocolate, a combination known as Mont Blanc.

Always crack and separate your eggs individually in a separate bowl, and transfer to the mixing bowl only when you're sure you've got just the egg white and no yolk or shell.

A rule of thumb is twice the amount of sugar to egg whites, consequently always weigh your egg whites as this will let you add the correct amount of sugar.

METHOD

1 Preheat the oven to 120°C.
2 Line a baking tray with greaseproof paper.
3 Ensure your mixing bowl, balloon whisky attachment, hands and worktop are clean as a whistle. To remove any trace of grease and make sure the bowl is in peak condition, wipe the bowl and whisk with a little of the vinegar or some lemon juice on kitchen paper.
4 Place the egg whites in the bowl and whisk until they form soft peaks – that is, they can just hold together as a point before collapsing back down.
5 Whisk in the sugar, one spoonful at a time. Finally add the cornflour and vinegar.
6 You should have a glossy, shiny mixture.
7 Take a dab of the mixture, dot the four corners of the baking tray and place your greaseproof paper on top. This will help to stick the paper to the tray.
8 Using a metal spoon, spoon the mixture on to the tray in equal-size portions, or make a single large disc for pavlova, or use as the recipe dictates.
9 Bake for ten minutes, then switch the oven off.
10 Leave the meringues in there for at least 3 hours, or even overnight, and don't open the door.

How to make buttercream

Buttercream is a versatile cake filling that can also be used to cover cakes entirely or as a topping. You'll have seen it on things like cupcakes and chocolate cakes. The key to a good buttercream is to use really good quality unsalted butter, so it's worth pushing the boat out a bit here. How you whip it is important too – you're after something really smooth, with no lumps or unmixed bits.

Besides the butter and icing sugar, you can also flavour and colour your buttercreams to make them more interesting to both eyes and taste buds. Fruit purées, food colourings, vanilla, coffee, booze and powdered chocolate can all be added to your buttercream once you've made the basic mix. You can either blend these flavours into a uniform colour, or it's quite the thing these days to roughly mix it in to give a sort of marbled effect; this works particularly well for things like raspberry purée or the zest of citrus fruits. Don't add too much liquid, though, as you'll dilute the mix.

I always think it's best to make more than you need with things like this (you can freeze any leftovers). The following amounts give you more than enough to cover and fill a standard 20cm/8in round cake.

INGREDIENTS

- 280g of unsalted butter at room temperature
- 560g of icing sugar
- 2 teaspoons of vanilla extract

METHOD

1 Beat the butter together with the vanilla until smooth and creamy. Put the mixer on its slowest setting and add a spoon of the icing sugar. Slowly add the rest one spoon at a time. This is to stop it blowing out of the bowl and all over your worktop.
2 Once it's all in, increase the speed to maximum for 30 seconds. Finally, add any other flavourings or colourings and combine.

How to make jelly

There is, to my mind at least, always something amusing about a wobbling jelly – it's just a fun ingredient. Go on, when was the last time you ate jelly? Well, though this book is about baking, and jellies aren't bakeable in the slightest, I wanted to include it as you can actually get pretty creative with jelly.

And they don't come more creative than Bompas & Parr, London's (if not the world's) only jellymongers. Sam Bompas and Harry Parr started playing with jelly in 2007, fusing art, food and architecture. They've now

produced works and events for some of the UK's biggest brands. They also have a range of adult flavours which are more akin to cocktails, such as 'Tacos & Tequila', which features coriander-infused Don Julio Silver, smoked pineapple, lime and salt; or 'Coral Cabana', made from raspberry jelly marbled into a Johnnie Walker Gold Label whisky sour.

The first jellies in the world would have been savoury, as well as sweet. This is because they would have been made from things like pigs' trotters. Sounds horrible to us, but savoury jellies were once a symbol of status. Achieving a clear, see-through jelly for your lord and master required a great deal of effort in the kitchen clarifying stock

to remove every last particle. Some savoury jellies even featured sugar, which back then was an expensive luxury and used in much the same way we might use vanilla.

But it was the Victorians, who we often think of as stiff and formal, who took jelly to the next level. They loved the stuff, and produced all sorts of fantastic moulds for making jelly in.

The best thing about jelly is that you can get creative with shapes and flavours. You

can, of course, buy packets of coloured jelly in the shops. However, if you want to get a little more experimental look out for leaf gelatine. The benefit of using this is that you can then set other liquids, such as fruit juices, fruit smoothies or custards. A rule of thumb is that four sheets of gelatine will set one pint/570ml of liquid, but if you're doing a large single mould err on the side of caution and use five.

METHOD

1 Whatever liquid you're trying to set needs to be warm, but mustn't boil. Do this first.
2 Soak the leaves of gelatine in cold water for five minutes.
3 Remove and squeeze out the excess water.
4 Place the rehydrated gelatine into your liquid and stir until it's completely dissolved.

5 Let the liquid cool down and pour into your moulds. Fill them three-quarters full.
6 Set in the fridge for 6 hours, or better still overnight.
7 To remove, run the tip of a knife dipped in boiling water around the edge and pull it away slightly from the mould with your fingers, then place on a plate and give the mould a good hard tap.

How to whip cream

Single, double, whipping, extra thick, sour, clotted and *crème fraîche* – there's a lot of different creams out there in the market place and they all have specific uses and roles. Here's what each cream is in the UK, as defined by law:

- Single cream – contains a minimum of 18% milk fat and is designed for pouring over puddings and cooking in sauces. It's too thin to ever whip, so don't try.
- Whipping cream – contains 35% fat, can be whipped and piped but is lighter than...
- Double cream – contains 48% fat, whips easily and can be piped.

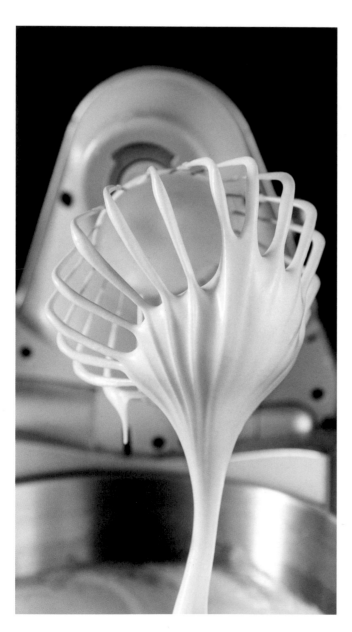

- Sour cream and *crème fraîche* are high-fat creams mixed with a souring bacterial culture to give a distinctive tang; both tend to be used mainly in savoury cooking, though sometimes in baking. The tartness can complement sweet dishes too.

Historically, dairymaids (and it normally was women) would leave the fresh milk to settle and the cream would rise to the top. This would then have to be carefully skimmed off. I remember milk being like this as a boy, until the invention of homogenisation, which saw the fat molecules from the cream beaten through all the milk. Milk is a 'colloid', which sees small globules of fat suspended in a water-based solution. By whipping cream you're creating a foam – air is being added and the movement of the whisk breaks down the fat molecules' protective membranes. Some of the air is then trapped by these membranes.

Because you're dealing with fat, you want your equipment to be as cool as possible. Consider putting the mixing bowl in the freezer for ten minutes. A hot kitchen with hot equipment will cause the fat in the cream to melt, which will release the air.

BY HAND OR IN A MIXER?

There's two schools of thought on this. By hand is more laborious, but gives you a tactile sense of when the cream is ready. Using a mixer is less effort, but there's a strong risk of over-mixing the cream. Cream can go from a thickish liquid to totally solid lump in just a few seconds, so if you are using an electric mixer watch it like a hawk and keep the speed lowish.

METHOD

1 Pour the cream into a large bowl.
2 If whisking by hand, tilt the bowl up slightly to pool the cream and begin whisking in a strong circular motion using a balloon whisk. I favour wire ones rather than the plastic ones.
3 If using a stand mixer or electric handheld whisk, pour the cream in the bowl and set the speed to slow. 500ml should be sufficiently whipped in just a few minutes.

Over-whisked cream will go firm, and will often clump around the whisk itself and start to split out the buttermilk – you're now well on the way to making butter. In fact this is exactly what you need to do to make soda bread (page 70). If this happens, (a) I told you so, and (b) you could try and rescue it by adding either some more fresh cream if you have some, or some milk.

How to make proper custard

Custard, a sauce so British even the French call it *crème anglaise*. It's the oil in the engine for the staple British pudding – our contribution to the baking world. If you're making apple pie (page 133) you've got to have custard. *Crème* is just custard that hasn't got itself together yet, while ice cream is just a frozen custard.

INGREDIENTS
- 300ml of full fat milk
- 3 egg yolks
- 4 tablespoons of caster sugar
- 1 vanilla pod or teaspoon of vanilla extract (optional)

Today, of course, reaching into the chiller cabinet you can grab a pot of single estate Madagascan vanilla custard made with free-range eggs and Fairtrade golden caster sugar for under £2. Oh how far we've come!

Making your own custard is dead easy, though – if you've got two eggs and some milk and sugar you're laughing.

METHOD
1 Put the milk in a pan, add the vanilla pod if using and bring up to a boil. Set aside and let the pod infuse in the milk.
2 After 20 minutes remove the pod and set aside to dry.
3 Whisk the eggs for a minute or two, then add the caster sugar and whisk for another 2–3 minutes until light yellow and fluffy. Add a small amount of the warm milk and mix gently.
4 Add the egg mix back to the warm milk and return to the hob on a low heat.
5 Keep stirring and after a few minutes the sauce will thicken. Serve straight away or keep on one side with a lid on to stop a skin forming.

THAT VANILLA POD
Vanilla pods aren't cheap, but they can be used three or four times. Another top tip is to put the pod in a sealed jar of caster sugar. The sugar takes on the flavour of the vanilla and can be used in the next custard you make.

EXTRA INGREDIENTS
Though we all think vanilla is the traditional flavouring in custard, history says otherwise. There are many older recipes that add things like cinnamon, lemon peel, brandy and peach water to increase the flavouring.

Working with chocolate

Chocolate, as I'm sure you know, is lovely stuff. Today there are some amazing chocolates available in the shops, which are a far cry from the brown fatty lard most people of my age grew up with. But choice can sometimes be bewildering, so here's a handy guide to which chocolate to use.

It all comes down to how much of the cocoa solids and cocoa butter are present, with most bars now displaying this percentage on their packaging. The higher the percentage, the more bitter it will be. However, often manufacturers combine the two figures to give an overall 'cocoa' figure. Other flavour factors to consider are where it was grown and how it was roasted and blended.

Chocolate with a higher cocoa content, say 70–85% can be used for baking, as most recipes counterbalance that bitterness with sugar. It will have a strong, dark flavour, however. So-called bitter-sweet chocolate contains around 60–70% cocoa solids, and as the name suggests has a balanced flavour making it a good all-rounder for most baking recipes.

Chocolate with 30–35% cocoa solids has a distinctly sweeter flavour. Milk chocolate varies between 20–40% cocoa solids and is best suited to light desserts requiring a more mild chocolate flavour.

Couverture chocolate is specifically made with a higher percentage of cocoa butter. This gives it a firmer snap when set and a glossy shine. It's the chocolate of choice for many professional chocolatiers and pastry makers. It's designed to be tempered and used to thinly coat cakes, hence its name (*couverture* means 'to cover').

TEMPERING CHOCOLATE

Tempering chocolate is the process of melting and cooling down the chocolate so that it'll look smooth and shiny when you dip items in it or pour in on things. If you don't do this correctly, the results can be strangely matt and dull-looking.

Break your chocolate into equal-sized pieces and put two-thirds in a bowl over a simmering pan of water. Melt it gently. Once it's melted, remove the bowl from the pan and add the remaining chocolate and stir. When this has been melted in it's ready to use.

MELTING CHOCOLATE

Low and slow is the way to melt chocolate, in a bowl over a pan of barely simmering water. Don't let the bowl touch the water. It helps if you break it up into small pieces first.

MAKING A GANACHE

Ganache is a smooth, pliable chocolate mixture often used to decorate cakes (or as the centre for chocolate truffles). For a standard 23cm cake, bring 225ml of double cream to the boil in a pan then add 350g of broken-up plain chocolate. Stir gently until the chocolate has melted. Leave somewhere cool to allow the mixture to thicken and set; then, using a palette knife, spread it over your cake.

MAKING CHOCOLATE CURLS FOR DECORATING CAKES

If you've got a large bar of chocolate and you only need a few fragments – for the centre of a cake, for example – simply flip the bar over and holding a chef's knife at a 90° angle, drag it along the back of the bar. You'll get shards and little curls that can be scattered over the top of a cake.

If you want bigger, more structured curls, melt the chocolate and pour on to a cool, clean work surface. Using a palette knife, spread it out gently and leave until it's just set. When it is, take your chef's knife and scrape it along the chocolate to make curls. You could try a potato peeler or cheese plane too.

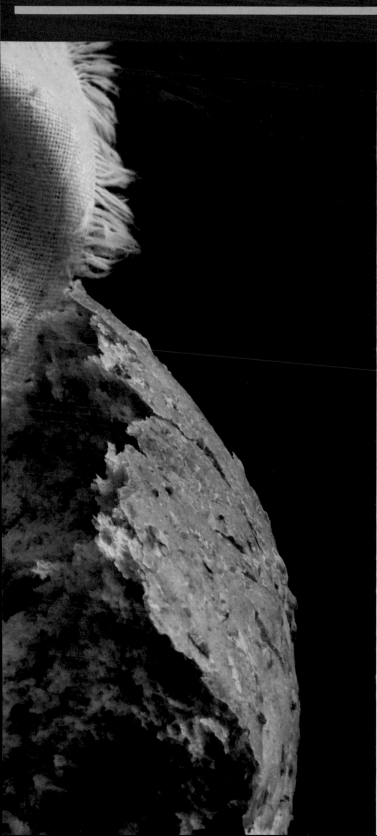

CHAPTER 3
SAVOURY THINGS

Bread. It's something most of us eat every day: toast for breakfast, sandwiches for lunch, garlic bread with dinner. Yet there *are* breads and real breads. Most bread in supermarkets is watery mass-produced rubbish, with no texture, crumb or flavour. Proper bread has taste, and needs nothing more than a smear of good butter to make it perfect.

Making bread, along with beer, used to be a mundane weekly household chore, much like vacuum-cleaning is today. Of course, nowadays we bake bread because we want to, not because we have to. Bread, I suppose, is a bit like chess: you can learn the rules fairly easily – after all, there's only a small set of ingredients to combine and cook – but to get really good at it takes practice, skill and dedication.

Easy white loaf

This loaf is a good one to start with if you're a complete beginner. It's worth spending a little time and effort to get this basic white bread dough right because from this, many different shapes of bread can be made.

INGREDIENTS

- 500g of strong white bread flour
- 7g of fast-action dried yeast
- 1 teaspoon of salt
- 1 tablespoon of vegetable oil
- 300ml of tepid water

METHOD

1. If you're using a stand mixer fit the dough hook. Otherwise, use your hands.
2. Place the flour in a large bowl and add the yeast and salt. Add the oil and then the water slowly and combine. Knead until the dough is smooth and elastic – about 10 minutes.
3. Wipe out the bowl and oil lightly with vegetable oil. Place the dough back in the bowl and cover with cling film.
4. Leave somewhere warm for 1 hour.
5. After an hour, or when the dough has risen, knock back with your fist and knead on a floured or oiled surface once more for a minute or two.
6. Shape into a circle with a twisting motion using the edges of your hands, and transfer to an oiled baking tray. Alternatively, place in a greased 1kg loaf tin.
7. Cover with a tea towel and leave to prove again for 30 minutes.
8. Preheat the oven to 180°C.
9. Using a very sharp knife or a craft knife, make three slashes in the top of the dough about 0.5cm deep.
10. Bake in the oven for around 35–40 minutes until the top is golden and the loaf sounds hollow when tapped on the base.
11. Leave to cool completely before cutting.

Brown loaf

This is very similar to the white loaf on the previous page, but using wholemeal flour. Wholemeal tends to be a little 'thicker' to work with; consequently you have to up the water amount. You can up the healthy option aspect even more by adding a handful of mixed seeds.

INGREDIENTS

- 500g of strong wholemeal bread flour
- 1 teaspoon of salt
- 1 teaspoon of quick yeast
- 1 tablespoon of vegetable oil
- 325ml of tepid water

METHOD

1 If you're using a stand mixer fit the dough hook, otherwise, use your hands.

2 Place the flour in a large bowl and add the yeast and salt. Add the oil and then the water slowly and combine. Add the seeds if using.

3 Knead until the dough is smooth and elastic – about 10 minutes by hand, less by machine.

4 Wipe out the bowl and oil lightly with more vegetable oil. Place the dough back in the bowl and cover with cling film.

5 Leave somewhere warm for 1 hour.

6 After an hour, or when the dough has risen, knock back with your fist and knead on a floured or oiled surface once more for a minute or two.

7 Shape into a circle with a twisting motion using the edges of your hands, and transfer to an oiled baking tray. Alternatively, place in a large greased 1kg loaf tin.

8 Cover with a tea towel and leave to prove again for 30 minutes.

9 Preheat the oven to 180°C.

10 Using a very sharp knife or a craft knife, make three slashes in the top of the dough about 0.5cm deep.

11 Bake in the oven for around 35–40 minutes until the top is golden and the loaf sounds hollow when tapped on the base.

12 Leave to cool completely before cutting.

Sourdough loaf

The king of breads as far as I'm concerned, sourdough has an honesty to it – historically, all bread was made like this, which is why the baker (along with the butcher and the candlestick maker) was such a key position in every town and village. The flavour isn't sour, it's more sharp. Indeed, some say a sourdough loaf will actually improve in flavour if left for a few days.

INGREDIENTS

For the sponge
- 200ml of your starter
- 250g of strong bread flour
- 300ml of tepid water

For the bread
- 300g of strong bread flour

Like many traditional ways of doing things, the main ingredients are time, planning and patience, plus flour, water, salt and your lovingly cared-for starter.

I'd recommend using a stand mixer fitted with a dough hook to make this. You *can* do it by hand, but it takes a lot longer than you think and makes more mess.

There are two stages to making a sourdough loaf. First you make what's called a sponge, which gets your starter up and running.

METHOD

1 8–10 hours before you want to start baking, make the sponge. Place the flour in a bowl. In a separate bowl, place the water, then add your starter. The starter should float on the water; if it sinks like a stone, it's not quite ready. Mix both together gently, cover in cling film and leave somewhere warm (you can do this overnight).

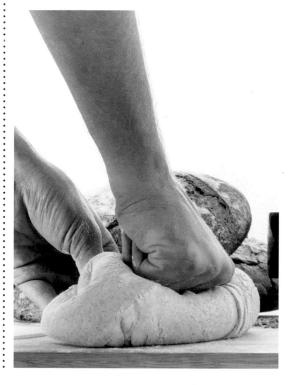

After 10 or more hours the sponge should be bubbling, and have a tangy aroma.

2 Add 300g of strong bread flour to the sponge and mix in a stand mixer, or by hand for 10–15 minutes. When the dough is smooth and has a dull shine, it's ready. Place in an oiled bowl and cover with cling film again and leave to prove for 3–4 hours.

3 Once the dough has risen again, knock it back gently using your knuckles to knock the air from it. You now need to shape it by hand and give it a second prove. To shape it, give it a knead on a floured surface and then tuck in the edges whilst twisting it 90°. This creates a 'bottom' and a smooth, strongly structured top.

4 Traditionally the second proving was done in cane baskets called bannetons; it's these that give the distinctive curling spiral on the top of sourdough loaves. If you've got one, gently place the dough 'bottom facing up' in the basket and leave to prove for another hour or more in a warm place. You don't have to use one, however, you could just use a bowl, or even a loaf tin.

5 When it's risen again, and you're ready to bake, turn the oven to a full whack 250°C or as hot as it'll go.

6 Get your pizza stone or baking tray in and hot, as well as another roasting tray under it. When the tray or stone is hot, dust with a little flour and, with a quick flick of the wrist, flip and tip your loaf out on to the tray. Slash the top three or four times with a scalpel or craft knife and place in the hot oven. Get a teacup of water and splash that in the roasting tray to create steam. Bake for 20 minutes at 230–250°C, then turn the oven down to 190°C and bake for another 20–30 minutes.

7 Don't be tempted to take it out as soon as the top goes golden – the middle will still be raw. You want it to develop a good dark crust. When you think it's ready, take out and leave to cool before slicing.

Ciabatta

While you might think that ciabatta is the sort of ancient bread enjoyed by the Romans, it was actually created in 1982. What's even more amazing is that it made landfall in the UK a mere three years later, when Marks & Spencer began stocking it in 1985. Perfect to munch on while Pavarotti sang *Nessun Dorma* for the World Cup in Italy in 1990.

INGREDIENTS
Makes two loaves

For the starter
- 150g of strong white flour
- 7g of fast-action yeast
- 150ml of warm water

For the dough
- 270g of strong white flour
- 1 teaspoon of salt
- 1 tablespoon of olive oil
- 7g of fast-action yeast
- 225ml of warm water
- 10g of semolina
- The starter you made previously

It was invented by Arnaldo Cavallari, a baker from Adria, near Venice. He and other bakers were concerned at the dominance of the French baguette in many sandwiches, as Italy didn't really have a bread you could load with a filling. So they set about developing one. It was soon a hit, and over the years new variations have sprung up – for instance in Rome it's often flavoured with marjoram.

Ciabatta dough is very wet. It's this moisture that gives it those large distinctive holes. However, because it's so wet it needs careful handling. It also has that distinctive shape, like a bow tie, with two fatter ends.

This is a loaf designed for filling, so be sure to load it up with meat, cheese, rocket, tomato and basil, drizzle with your best olive oil and wrap snugly to allow the flavours to marry.

Ciabatta is best made in two stages. Firstly you make what's called the starter, or *biga*, the night before. The next day you use this to make the actual dough. You don't want to knead the dough too much, as you'll knock all the air out, and air bubbles are what will give you those lovely big holes. When handling, don't be tempted to add more flour. Instead keep your hands wet, as this will stop the dough from sticking.

METHOD

1. First make the starter.
2. Mix all the dry ingredients in a bowl and add the warm water to make a smooth batter as thick as double cream. Cover with cling film or a clean tea towel and leave somewhere warmish (by the kettle, say) overnight. In the morning it should be full of bubbles.
3. When you're ready to make the bread fit the dough hook to your mixer. Add the flour and the yeast to the bowl, then the salt, oil and starter. Finally add the water. Turn the mixer on low and gently mix together. When fully combined increase the speed a little to medium, which will help develop the gluten.
4. The dough will gradually thicken and start to come away from the sides of the bowl. When it does, transfer to your largest bowl, which you've lightly oiled, and set aside somewhere warm to prove. It should triple in size in about 2 hours depending on how warm your kitchen is.
5. Preheat your oven to full whack, 250°C, and get a large baking sheet, or even better a pizza stone, hot too.
6. When ready, don't knock it back, but transfer it to a well-dusted bench. Cut in half and stretch out to an oblong shape (ciabatta is Italian for slippers, though you'd have to have serious feet to have something like this as your shoe). Dust with a little flour and leave to prove for another 30 minutes.
7. Dust the hot baking tray or pizza stone with flour or semolina and transfer the loaves to it. Place in the hot oven and spritz with water or splash a little on the bottom to create some steam. Close the door and bake for 25–30 minutes until the ciabattas have risen up and sound hollow when the bottom is tapped.

Focaccia

Unlike the young upstart ciabatta, focaccia is over 2,000 years old. The name comes from *focus*, meaning hearth, and this is where the bread would have been baked. Today there are many regional variations in Italy, but the most common 'white focaccia' features rosemary, salt crystals and olive oil. It differs from pizza dough in that it uses more yeast, giving a greater rise and looser crumb. This allows it to absorb the olive oil.

INGREDIENTS

- 2 teaspoons of quick-action yeast
- 2 tablespoons of good olive oil
- 400g of strong white flour
- 250ml of tepid water

For the topping

- 1–2 tablespoons of extra virgin olive oil
- Handful of rosemary sprigs
- Pinch of dried oregano
- 2 teaspoons of sea salt

METHOD

1 Oil a shallow baking tray around 20cm x 25cm and set aside. Snip sprigs of rosemary off the branch and into a bowl of water.

2 Put the yeast, water, salt and flour in a bowl and mix with a dough hook on a stand mixer. Alternatively use your fingers like claws and combine to form a soft dough which should come away from the sides of the bowl.

3 Turn out and knead for ten minutes until the dough is smooth.

4 Wipe out the bowl and oil lightly with vegetable oil. Place the dough back in the bowl and cover with cling film.

5 Leave somewhere warm for 1 hour.

6 After an hour, or when the dough has risen, knock back with your fist and knead once more for a minute or two.

7 Roll into a rectangle shape about 1.5cm thick and a little smaller than your baking tray.

8 Brush the top of the dough with olive oil, and then using your fingertips punch impressions into the dough at regular intervals. Quickly tuck a sprig of rosemary in each hole as you make them.

9 Place in a large proving bag, or cover with oiled cling film and leave to prove again for around 30 minutes.

10 Preheat the oven to 170°C.

11 Remove from proving bag and brush once more with oil, and scatter over the sea salt.

12 Bake in the oven for around 20–25 minutes until golden brown.

13 Cut into squares or soldiers and serve warm.

The key thing with making focaccia is to first soak the rosemary sprigs, and secondly to tuck them snugly down into the dough. This not only stops them burning, it also allows their flavour to permeate the dough.

Fougasse

Historically fougasse was the bread Continental bakers used to judge the temperature and readiness of the wood-fired oven before loading in the rest of the bread. It was probably also their lunch.

INGREDIENTS

- 500g of strong white flour
- 350ml of warm water
- 7g of fast-action yeast
- 1 teaspoon of salt
- 1 tablespoon of semolina flour

METHOD

1 Combine the yeast, salt and flour and add the water. Mix together using your fingers and once the dough has come together, transfer to your work surface. Knead the dough for 10 minutes by stretching it away from you and repeatedly folding over. You know it's ready when it doesn't stick any more and develops a shine. You can also do all of this in a mixer fitted with a dough hook. Lastly, add the olives and give it a final knead.

2 Wipe out the mixing bowl and add a little olive oil. Shape the dough into a ball, place back in the bowl, cover with a tea towel or cling film and leave to prove for 1 hour. Lightly oil a baking tray. (Depending on the size of your tray, you might need two.)

3 Set your oven to full whack, 220°C.

4 Dust your bench with the semolina flour and tip the dough on to the surface. Roughly shape into a rectangle and divide the dough into three strips. Transfer to the oiled baking tray.

5 Using your plastic scraper, cut a line from the centre of each strip up and down, but not all the way to the edge.

6 Either side of that central cut, make three more cuts, again not all the way to the edge of the dough.

7 Using your hands, shape out into the traditional fougasse petal shape. Repeat with the other two strips.

8 Place in the oven and bake for 10–15 minutes. Just after you put it in, open the oven door and throw in some water to create some steam.

Fougasse is great as it is, but you can also get creative with extra ingredients mixed into the dough. Olives are a popular one, but lardons, cheese, seeds and nuts can all be added too. Any extra flavours or ingredients are best kneaded in after the dough has first risen.

Soda bread

Soda bread is most commonly associated with Ireland, but you'd be wrong to think it has a long and rich history there. Soda bread is leavened not by the ancient method of using yeast, but by using bicarbonate of soda, which became more readily available in Ireland in the middle of the 18th century.

INGREDIENTS
Makes one loaf

- 225g of plain flour
- 225g of wholewheat flour
- 1 teaspoon of salt
- 1 teaspoon of bicarbonate of soda
- 450ml of buttermilk

Prior to that, Ireland like the UK grew 'soft' wheat, which had a low gluten level and produced flattish breads such as farls. Furthermore, despite having this wonderfully modern ingredient produced by chemists and scientists, soda bread was traditionally marked with a cross to 'ward off the devil' – superstition and science in one bite. A more secular school of thought is that this helps the bread cook more quickly. Traditionally it was cooked in a metal pot with a lid over a peat fire, rather than baked in an oven.

The other key ingredient in soda bread is buttermilk, which contains lactic acid that reacts with the soda to produce carbon dioxide, causing the loaf to rise.

Soda bread is an absolute doddle to make once you've got the ingredients, and can be rustled up in the time it takes for someone to phone and say 'I'll be over in 20 minutes'. Just don't overwork the dough, though – it doesn't even need kneading, just sort of bringing together really. I like to keep things simple with soda bread, but if you'd rather up the wholemeal flour

or throw in a handful of oats, be my guest, this is a bread that can take a fair bit of customisation.

METHOD

1. Preheat oven to 200°C.
2. Sieve the flours, salt and bicarbonate of soda into a large bowl. Make a well in the centre and pour in 400ml of the buttermilk at first. Using one hand, slowly bring the mixture together; add some more of the buttermilk if you think it needs it (if you're using all wholemeal flour it may want even more, as wholemeal is more absorbent than white flour).
3. When combined, turn out on to a lightly floured bench and gently shape into a cylinder. Using a knife or a dough scraper make a cross shape on the loaf.
4. Place on an oiled baking tray and straight into the oven. Bake for 45 minutes. It's done when it's golden brown and sounds slightly hollow when tapped on the bottom.
5. If you want a hard crust, leave to cool on a wire rack. You can achieve a soft crust by wrapping the warm loaf in a clean tea towel and leaving to cool.

MAKE YOUR OWN BUTTER TOO

If you're making your own bread, why not make your own butter to serve with it? It's not as hard as you think:

1. Take two cartons of buttermilk and pour into a food mixer fitted with a balloon whisk attachment (the blades of a hand mixer are too flat and sharp). Fire it up but watch it carefully.
2. After about 10 minutes the solids in the buttermilk will start to form in the centre of the balloon whisk. That is butter. To remove any excess water, wrap in kitchen roll and press between two chopping boards.
3. The leftover milky water can still be used to make soda bread – just make sure you've got enough. You might need to top up with ordinary milk soured with lemon juice.

Rye bread

Rye flour is becoming increasingly popular in the UK these days, and with its nutty taste it's easy to see why. Primarily associated with Northern Europe and Scandinavian countries, rye has less gluten that wheat flour, so the resulting loaves are heavier in weight. I've cut the rye flour with a little wheat flour in this recipe, just to help things along.

INGREDIENTS
- 400g of rye flour
- 100g of strong white flour
- 7g of fast-action yeast
- ½ teaspoon of salt
- 300ml of warm water
- 1 tablespoon of honey or black treacle
- Caraway seeds (optional)

With a nod to its heritage, rye is best paired with things like salmon, salt beef, fish, cream cheese, pastrami, sausages and sauerkraut, rather than rocket and sun-dried tomatoes.

METHOD

1 Put the flours into a large mixing bowl and add the yeast and the salt. Add the honey to the warm water and stir to dissolve, then pour over the flour and yeast.

2 Using your fingers like a claw, bring the dough together until combined and coming away from the sides of the bowl. Then transfer to a floured worktop.

3 Knead the dough for five minutes by stretching and shaping it.

4 Wipe out the mixing bowl with kitchen paper and lightly oil.

5 Place the dough back in the bowl and cover with cling film or a clean tea towel and leave somewhere warmish for an hour to double in size. Oil and flour-line a 2lb/900g loaf tin.

6 Remove from the bowl and knead again briefly before forming into a lozenge shape. Place in the tin and leave to settle and prove again for another 30 minutes. Alternatively shape into a ball and place in an oiled and floured cake tin.

7 Preheat the oven to 200°C.

8 Bake for around 30 minutes until the top is crisp and brown. Remove and leave to cool slightly before removing from the tin and place in the switched-off oven for five minutes just to firm up the sides.

Brioche burger buns

Unless you've been living in a cave for the past five years, or perhaps detained at Her Majesty's pleasure, you'll know that proper burgers, pulled pork and 'dude food' is now officially 'A Thing'.

INGREDIENTS
Makes around a dozen buns

- 300g of strong bread flour
- 30g of caster sugar
- 5g of salt
- 2 teaspoons of dried instant yeast
- 70ml of warm milk
- 3 medium eggs
- 100g of butter, cut into cubes at room temperature

For the egg wash
- 1 egg, beaten
- 40ml of milk

You'll also know that putting your home-made burgers or meat on any old floury bap is a schoolboy error only chain pubs and fast food outlets make. No, if you're going to do it properly it's got to be on brioche buns.

Now, while I have occasionally seen these in supermarkets, and at my local bakers, they're not widely available. Thankfully it's not that hard to make your own, and if you've gone to the trouble of buying really good burgers from the butchers, or even making your own (ground beef and seasoning, squashed in a burger press is all it takes), then it's a bit of a crime to put it in a rubbish bun.

Now, traditional brioche is a bread heavily enriched with egg and butter, giving it a bright golden colour. It's often eaten for breakfast. For brioche burger buns, however, we don't want too much butter, as this can cause a soggy bottom when your hot burger hits the bread.

METHOD

1 In a stand mixer fitted with a dough hook, place the egg, milk, sugar and yeast and mix on a low speed until well mixed and the sugar has dissolved. Add the salt and the flour in small amounts. Once it's all in and combined, add the butter and keep mixing for around 20 minutes until the dough comes cleanly away from the sides of the bowl and is light and elastic.

2 Add a little vegetable oil to a clean bowl and transfer the dough to it. Cover with cling film and leave to prove for 1–3 hours depending on how warm your kitchen is.

3 Once proved, knock it back and knead by hand again for a few minutes. Roll out into a sausage and, using scissors, cut in half, then cut each half in half, then cut each of those four pieces into three. These will be your buns.

Shaping the buns

4 There's a bit of a knack to doing this. Slightly flatten each piece and then fold the edges into the centre. Turn the dough over, so the seam is on the underside, and give a little roll around to even out. You want 12 nicely shaped balls of dough around 80g in weight.

5 Transfer to a baking tray lined with baking parchment and cover with a piece of lightly oiled cling film. Leave for another hour or so to prove again.

6 Preheat the oven to 180°C and place a small baking tray filled with a little water in the bottom of the oven.

7 Just before placing the buns in the oven make the egg wash by combining the egg and milk. Then, using a pastry brush, lightly brush the top of each bun. This would be the time to add any sesame seeds if you want that look. Place in the oven for about 15 minutes.

8 You can do all this the day before your barbecue. Just keep the buns in an airtight container.

Flat breads and chapatis

Possibly the easiest bread in the world to make, and good with everything from couscous to curry. Breads like this must be as old as agriculture. They would be made in the morning, to have for breakfast with yoghurt or fruit. You can use wholemeal flour for this, or just make a visit to any Indian supermarket and you'll find chapati flour.

INGREDIENTS
- 300g of wholemeal or chapati flour
- Around 200ml of warm water
- Pinch of salt
- Four tablespoons of melted butter or ghee

METHOD
1 Put the flour and salt in a large bowl and add the water. Using your hand like a claw, combine to form a dough. Turn out on to a lightly floured worktop and knead for 10 minutes.

2 Wipe out the bowl and grease with a little oil, and place the dough back in the bowl. Cover it with cling film or a tea towel, and leave to relax for no more than 30 minutes.

3 Get a shallow, dry frying or pancake pan ready on the hob. Have a clean tea towel standing by to keep your cooked chapatis in.

4 When you're ready to make them, remove the dough and roll out into a sausage shape. Cut into discs around 2cm in diameter and dredge in a little spare flour. Roll out the first disc into a circle about 6–7cm in diameter, and place on the hot pan.

5 Turn after a few minutes – you don't want them to burn, but a bit of colour is OK.

6 If they puff up, which they may do, that's OK. Just gently squash down with a clean tea towel.

7 When done, remove and brush with a little melted butter or ghee and tuck under the tea towel to keep warm.

8 As you get the hang of this you'll find you can get a little production line going, turning out bread after bread.

Crumpets

Now that you can buy crumpets in the shops few people make their own any more. Why is that? You can buy versions of nearly all the breads and cakes in this book in the shops too, but people still want to bake them. Yet when it comes to crumpets, people think 'Nah, too much bother'. Well, nothing good ever came easy, and you're the type of chap who likes a challenge, right?

INGREDIENTS

- 250g of strong bread flour
- 100g of plain flour
- 7g of fast action yeast
- 2 teaspoons of sugar
- 350ml of warm milk
- 200ml of warm water
- 1 teaspoon of salt
- 1 teaspoon of baking powder
- Neutral oil for cooking (and spreading on afterwards)

To make crumpets properly you need to invest in a set of crumpet rings. You'll also need as flat a pan as possible. Actually, what we now think of as a crumpet, with all its little butter-absorbing holes, is in fact a Victorian invention made possible by baking powder. Prior to that they were more like pancakes or drop scones.

I make these in a stand mixer, but you could use an electric hand whisk. You'll also need a crumpet ring, and I'd recommend a shallow-sided pancake pan with a flat bottom.

METHOD

1 Warm the milk in the microwave and make up the warm water with a bit from the kettle topped up with cold water. Place the flours, yeast and sugar in the bowl and turn the machine on. Add the milk, slowly at first, and then add the water bit by bit. (You might not need all of it.) Keep mixing until you've something a little thicker than double cream or pancake batter.

2 Leave to rest for over an hour in the bowl.

3 Get the pan on the hob on the lowest heat it can do, place the crumpet ring on it and add a little oil using a pastry brush. Smear the oil up the sides of the ring too, to prevent sticking.

4 After an hour the mixture should be really bubbly. Beat the salt and the baking powder into the batter and mix quickly. Thin down with a little water.

5 Take the bowl over to the hob. Using a ladle, slowly spoon out enough of the batter to half fill the ring. Ideally the batter should be thick enough not to leak out from under the tiny gap between the pan and the ring. If it does, thicken your batter with a bit more strong flour.

6 Cook for longer than you think – you should see telltale tiny bubbles start to form. Once these have stopped forming, and the top goes from shiny to matt in appearance, your crumpet should be ready. Lift the ring from the pan and remove the crumpet. If it's stuck in places, cut free with a sharp knife.

7 Repeat using up the rest of the batter. You can also make these on a sandwich toaster if you've got one.

8 Once cool you can freeze your crumpets, or toast them again. I like three of them, smothered with butter and a scraping of Gentleman's Relish. That chaps, is a salty, fatty, carb hat-trick right there.

Meet the crumpizza

It turns out that when you've only got one crumpet ring, making six or more crumpets takes a while. 'So why not cook one huge crumpet, and serve it in slices like a pizza?' I thought. Thus was born the crumpizza.

© Helen Graves CC BY-SA 2.0.

Fool's gold loaf

I've included this more out of curiosity and as a piece of social history than for any other reason – I'm not saying that you should try and make it. So, are you ready? Here's the story. OK, at some point we've all had a case of the late-night munchies, right? But when you're Elvis Presley a Twix and a bag of crisps from the 24-hour garage just isn't going to cut it.

INGREDIENTS
- 1 large flattish soft white loaf
- 1 jar of smooth peanut butter
- 1 jar of grape jam (or blueberry, or plum)
- 450g of smoked streaky bacon

On the evening of 1 February 1970 Elvis was at home in Graceland, Tennessee, with the two Denver police personnel, Captain Jerry Kennedy and Ron Pietrafeso. They were friends with Cindy and Buck Scott, who owned the Colorado Mine Company restaurant in Denver and had invented this sandwich. The name comes from the fact it cost nearly $50 at the time.

They started discussing the sandwich, and apparently Elvis decided he wanted one there and then. They flew in his private jet to Denver, where Cindy and Buck met them at the airport with 22 of the sandwiches. They washed them down with champagne and mineral water. That's a distance of over 1,000 miles and a two-hour flight. To put that in some sort of UK perspective, it's like sitting in London and saying 'Say, fellers, I could murder a currywurst' and flying to Berlin. You've got to hand it to The King, he did things with style...

So, what's in it? Well, here's what you need:

METHOD
1. Cook the bacon under the grill until crisp, dry with kitchen paper, and set aside to cool.
2. Slice the loaf in two horizontally and remove most of the crumb.
3. Toast lightly under the grill.
4. Spread as much peanut butter as possible on the bottom layer.
5. Place the bacon on the peanut butter.
6. Spread as much jam as possible on the underside of the top layer.
7. Squash firmly together.
8. Cut into slices and serve. Should be sufficient for 6–8 people. Or The King.

Pizza

Originating in Naples, pizza started out as a cheap and popular snack for the poor. When Count Charles Arrivabene visited Italy in the 1860s, he commented 'pizza is a sort of dry cake made of flour, garlic and oil, a horrid composition of which nevertheless the Italians of the South are particularly fond'. So like burgers and fish and chips, pizza started life as poor people's food. It didn't arrive in Britain until the late 1950s, when a few pizza restaurants opened in Soho.

INGREDIENTS

Enough for 4 to 6 pizzas depending on how big you roll them out.

For the dough

- 500g of strong white bread flour
- 100g of finely ground semolina flour
- 3 teaspoons of fast action yeast
- Large pinch of salt
- 300ml of warm water
- 4 tablespoons of olive oil

For the tomato sauce

- 1 can of plum tomatoes (not the pre-chopped ones, which tend to be more watery)
- Pinch of oregano
- 1 clove of garlic

Toppings

- Diced or grated mozzarella cheese plus whatever you fancy – pepperoni, mushrooms, ham (not pineapple!), olives, salmon, spinach (wilt and drain it first).

By the 1980s there were Pizza Express, Pizza Hut (opened 1973) and Pizza Land, where in 1975 49p got you two slices of pizza and a jacket potato! Like chips instead of rice with curry, we sometimes don't get other nations' food right at first.

To cook pizza properly you need to get your oven full whack, maximum warp hot. Most ovens go up to about 210–230°C, whereas a wood-fired pizza oven can easily get to 300–350°C. However, there are clips on the Internet of people hacking their ovens' thermostats to get them even hotter (I don't recommend this).

If you like pizza, and who doesn't, then invest in a pizza stone (page 21). One of these will give you that dry, chewy crust that good pizzas should have. You can get them for around a tenner. Always get them as hot as the oven before placing your pizza on them. You can use a thick baking tray, or even your grill pan turned upside down, but stones are best.

METHOD

1 Put the flour and 80g of the semolina in a large bowl and add the salt on one side and the yeast on the other. Make a well in the centre, add the oil, then slowly add the water and start to bring together.

2 Keep mixing until the dough has come together and the sides of the bowl are relatively clean. Then transfer on to a floured work surface.

3 Knead for 5 to 10 minutes as hard as you can manage by stretching out the dough away from you and folding it back over. Then turn 15° and repeat. When it's well kneaded, shape into a ball using your dough scraper and check to see if it's ready by prodding it. If the dough springs back, it's ready.

4 Wash and dry your mixing bowl and add another tablespoon of olive oil to it and smear around the sides.

5 Place the dough in the bowl, cover with cling film or a damp cloth, and leave in a warm kitchen to prove for about an hour, after which it should have doubled in size.

6 While it's proving, make your sauce and get your toppings ready.

7 Put the sauce ingredients into a jug or high-sided saucepan, and, using a stick blender, blitz to a smooth sauce. Alternatively you can do this step in a food blender. In the past I used to cook pizza sauces prior to using on the base, but one day was pushed for time and did it this way, and the results were just as good. You can simmer it, perhaps with some diced, fried onion if you prefer. Get any toppings you're using out of their packets, on to a board and ready to use.

Made to measure

8 I have a huge 40cm x 40cm wooden chopping board from Ikea that I place my 33cm pizza stone on and, using a knife or large nail, scratch around it. This lets me know how big the stone is so I don't accidentally roll a shape that's too big for the stone.

9 Dust your bench or board with semolina flour and cut a cricket-ball sized piece dough from the rest in the bowl and begin to roll out into a circle.

10 With your oven glowing white hot and your hands in your thickest oven gloves, remove the pizza stone (remembering to close the oven door), and, using your rolling pin, transfer the pizza base on to it.

11 Working quickly, place around two tablespoons of sauce on the base and smooth around to cover – leave a gap of about 2cm round the edge. Apply your toppings then top with a handful of cheese. Drizzle over a little olive oil and slam back in the oven.

12 It should take about 10 minutes, depending on how hot your oven is. It's ready when the base has puffed up a little and the cheese is all melted and golden. Let it rest a few minutes before you try and cut into wedges with a pizza wheel.

Pissaladiere

Originally from Nice in the south of France, this tart featuring onions and anchovies helps work up a thirst and is great for picnics. The trick to making a good one is in the onions – you have to cook them right down, on a low heat so they soften, caramelise and become sweeter rather than acidic. This process can take over 20 minutes, and you'll need to keep stirring them so that they don't stick to the pan.

Still, what's better than pottering around the kitchen with pastry and onions?

INGREDIENTS

- 3 large onions
- 20g of butter
- Pinch of sea salt
- 2 tablespoons of vegetable oil
- 1 375g packet of puff pastry
- 1 jar or tin of anchovies
- 1 jar of black olives, drained and halved

METHOD

1 Cut the onions in half and peel off the outer layers. Chop off the tip, and slice the rest of the onion thinly down to the root, which you can throw away.

2 Put the oil and butter in a pan and put on a low heat. Add the onions and a pinch of salt and stir to coat in the melted butter and oil. Leave it ticking over, stirring occasionally. You do not want the onions to brown, just soften and turn golden.

3 When they're ready, turn out the heat and leave to cool.

4 Preheat the oven to 180°C.

5 Open and drain the anchovies – give them a quick rinse under a cold tap. Carefully split each anchovy in half and set aside.

6 Take the puff pastry from the fridge and roll out on a baking tray to a rectangle.

7 Using a knife, score a line 1cm in from the edge of the pastry to form a border, being careful not to cut through the pastry.

8 Spread the onion mix over the pastry and smooth down with a palette knife.

9 Take your halved anchovy fillets and make a criss-cross lattice design on top of the onion.

10 Add an olive in each 'diamond' made by the anchovies.

11 Grind some black pepper over it (it won't need any salt!) and bake in the oven for around 25 minutes until the pastry is golden.

Sausage rolls

Home-made sausage rolls still warm from the oven with a blob of English mustard and a glass of good beer are about as good a snack as a chap can hope for. Poorly-made, cheap commercial ones, on the other hand, are 'orrible. It's the way they coat the roof of your mouth with that claggy film, and the way they don't really taste of anything.

INGREDIENTS
For the filling
- 6 or 8 good-quality sausages
- 1 pack of ready rolled puff pastry
- One small finely grated onion (or you could blitz in a food processor) – alternatively finely dice it and fry it gently in a little oil before adding to the sausage meat.
- Any herbs you fancy – finely chopped sage is nice, you could also add diced apricot, or nutmeg, onion marmalade, more salt and pepper, curry powder, grated cheese, anything really, except perhaps Space Dust (now *there's* an idea!)

Cheat by buying really good bangers, squeezing out the meat, and pimping it up with a few flavoursome extras.

METHOD
1 Squeeze the meat from your sausages into a bowl and add any extras you're using. Add the onion and mix well. Tip out on to a board and roll back into three sausage shapes about 4cm thick.
2 Unroll your pastry and cut lengthways into three long strips about 8cm wide.
3 Preheat the oven to 200°C.
4 Place each sausage-meat piece on a strip of pastry lengthways and roll the pastry over, sealing with beaten egg. Roll each cylinder on the bench to ensure a nice, round, sealed shape, then place with the edge facing down on a non-stick baking tray. Brush with the remaining egg wash, and pop in the hot oven for about 20 minutes until the pastry is golden brown. Serve with mustard, curry or chilli sauce and a few beers.

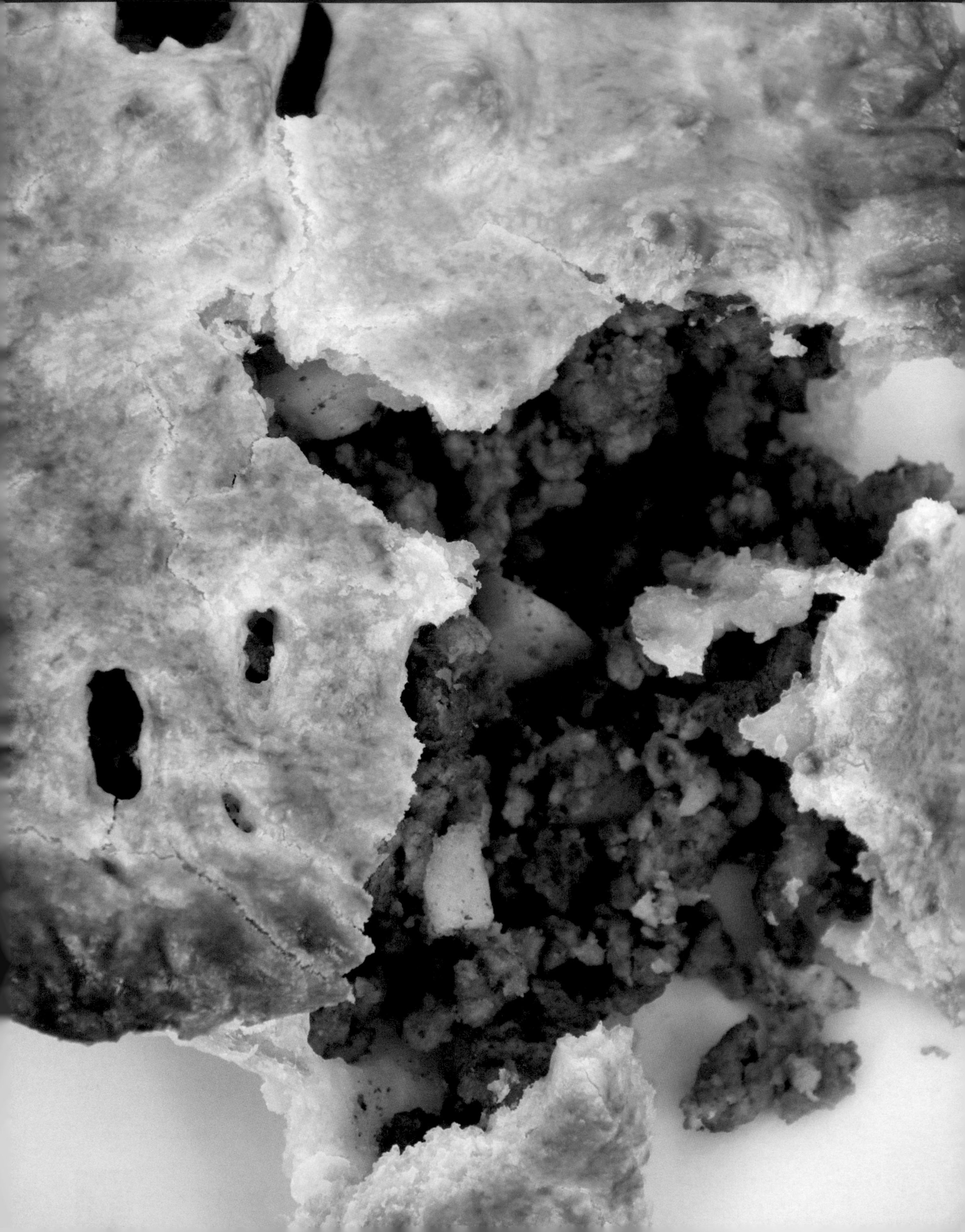

Meat pies

I can't think of a cheaper beef pie than this. It also happens to be dead easy to make. The filling is similar to that used in a cottage pie. My advice is to bulk buy some good quality mince, make a huge vat of this, and freeze into portions. You can then whip it out and encase in freshly made pastry.

INGREDIENTS
- 500g of beef mince
- 200ml of beef stock
- 2 onions
- Tablespoon of vegetable oil
- 1 stick of celery
- 1 carrot
- Large handful of frozen peas (optional)
- Salt and pepper
- 1 teaspoon of tomato purée

For the pastry
- 400g of plain flour
- 100g of butter
- 100g of lard
- Pinch of salt
- A few tablespoons of cold water
- 1 beaten egg or milk to seal the edge and glaze

This is for a large 9in/23cm double crust pie. The filling would make three to four individual pies. For a single crust pie you won't need as much pastry (freeze the leftover), but you may need a pie bird.

METHOD
To make the filling
1 Bring your meat out of the fridge and remove from the packet; pat dry with kitchen roll if necessary. Chop your onions, carrots and celery into a dice (you can use other diced vegetables such as swede, parsnip or potato to bulk out your pie).
2 On a highish heat, add the oil to the pan and begin browning the mince in small batches. Only move it when it starts to brown and comes away easily. When browned nearly all over, remove to a side plate.
3 When all the mince is done, add the vegetables and cook in any remaining fat or oil until the onion is translucent (about 8–10 minutes). Add the tomato purée, the stock and the meat and any juices back to the pan and combine. Add the seasoning and simmer, lid off, for 30 minutes, stirring occasionally.

4 When the filling is thickened and reduced you can remove from the heat. If your filling looks a little runny, blend a teaspoon of cornflour in cold water and add to thicken it.
5 Add the peas if you want to – these will cook in the residual heat as well as when baked in the pie. Let the filling cool right down before you try to fill a pie case with it. It's at this stage that you can freeze it.

To make the pastry
6 While your filling is cooling down make the pastry. Make the shortcrust in the method described on page 44. Chill, then roll out to fit your tin. Combine the leftovers if you need to and re-roll out to cut your pie lids.
7 Add the filling to the lined pastry case to just over three-quarters full – you don't want to overfill it. Brush the lip with beaten egg and pop the lid on. Crimp with your fingers or a fork to get a good seal. Brush with the beaten egg and put in a preheated oven at 180°C for 25–30 minutes until the crust looks golden brown.
8 Take out and let cool a little before serving.

CHAPTER 4
SWEET BREADS AND LARGE CAKES

Like a village fete cake stand, what follows is a selection of my favourite large, round cakes. There are classics like Victoria sponge and lemon drizzle, as well as the more unusual like orange and saffron cake. These are cakes for cutting and sharing. What's more, they'll all keep for a few days if kept somewhere cool. The richer fruit cakes, meanwhile, will keep for months. It's worth investing in some decent tins and plastic boxes to store your efforts, and next time you get a tin of chocolates at Christmas, hold on to the tin.

Victoria sponge

Right, this is it, gents. The easiest cake in the world. Master this and the world's your oyster. The beauty of a basic sponge mix like this is that it's a blank canvas for other flavours, so you try experimenting with extra ingredients like cocoa, coffee or caramel. Also, many of the other round, two-tiered cakes in this book are made in a similar method.

INGREDIENTS
- 4 medium eggs (should weigh around 220g) 220g of plain flour
- 220g of unsalted butter at room temperature
- 220g of caster sugar
- 2 teaspoons of vanilla extract
- 3 teaspoons of baking powder
- 3–4 tablespoons of jam for the filling

For the buttercream
- 100g of unsalted butter at room temperature
- 200g of icing sugar
- Splash of milk

Few cakes are more iconically English than a Victoria sandwich; red jam, white cream, tea, village fetes, Spitfires, warm beer, stiff upper lip, jumpers for goal posts... England. There were many things named after the iconic monarch in her lifetime, but the Victoria sandwich, or sponge, remains the best known. Queen Victoria famously had rather a sweet tooth, and loved cake. She would have cakes from the kitchens at Buckingham Palace sent to either Balmoral or Osborne House on the Isle of Wight.

And it is another famous Victorian woman that we must thank for the recipes – a young journalist and author who tragically died at the age of just 28, one Mrs Beeton. The first written recipe for the cake appears in her eponymous tome, though as it's generally thought she plagiarised many of the recipes in her book, it may have existed earlier elsewhere.

Beeton's original recipe calls for four eggs, and their weight in sugar, butter, and flour, and that tip is as true today as it was then.

METHOD
1 Preheat the oven to 170°C.
2 Place a cake tin on a piece of baking parchment and score round it with the tip of a very sharp knife. Grease and line your cake tins.
3 Place a bowl on the scales and reset to zero. Crack the eggs into the bowl and note the weight.
4 Place another bowl on the scales and reset. Weigh out the same weight of butter (or just go for 220g) and cut into small cubes.
5 Place the butter in the bowl of a stand mixer, or, if beating by hand, leave in the bowl.
6 Weigh out the sugar and add to the butter. Mix until light and fluffy.
7 Add the eggs to the butter, and weigh out the flour. Add this gradually too.
8 Add the vanilla extract, and last of all the baking powder.
9 Divide the mixture between two cake tins and smooth over with a spatula or palette knife.
10 Place in the oven and bake for 20 minutes.
11 Test with a metal skewer, and if it comes out clean the cakes are done.
12 Leave to cool for 5 minutes before removing from the tins and peeling off the baking parchment.
13 While it's cooling make the buttercream. Beat the butter until it's light and fluffy, then add the sugar. Loosen with a drop of milk or two. Set aside.
14 When cool, select one cake for the bottom half and, using a bread knife, cut the very topmost crust off to get it level if it's too domed. Spread the jam on this, spread the buttercream on the jam and place the second cake on top.
15 Dust with icing sugar and gaze upon your works, ye mighty!

Banana bread

Conventional wisdom says you shouldn't even think about attempting this recipe unless your bananas are on their way to being black as the ace of spades, as it's just not possible to make good banana bread with green straight-from-the-supermarket bananas. And I'd second that. However, where there's a will there's a way, and if your bananas are a little on the green side, you can turbo ripen them in the oven. Place on a sheet of baking parchment (this is in case they burst or leak) and bake in a 150°C oven for 30 to 40 minutes. This should send the outsides black and soften up the insides ready for banana bread. You can, of course, fly in the face of conventional wisdom and use green bananas, they'll just be a bit harder to mash.

INGREDIENTS

- 150g of butter
- 150g of golden caster sugar
- 200g of plain flour
- 3 teaspoons of baking powder
- 3 ripe bananas
- 1 teaspoon of salt
- 2 eggs, beaten
- Handful of dried banana chips blitzed in food processor (optional)

In 1999 archaeologists digging on the site of the new City Hall in London found an unpeeled banana during an excavation of a Tudor rubbish dump, dating it to somewhere in the middle of the 16th century. Yet it was only at the turn of the last century that someone thought to add bananas to a cake mix.

I've turned the banana flavour up to 11 in this recipe by adding chips of freeze-dried bananas. You can omit them if you like, or replace with a handful of chopped nuts.

METHOD

1 Preheat oven to 160°C.

2 Grease a 2lb loaf tin with butter and line with baking parchment. In a stand mixer, cream the butter and sugar together until light and fluffy. Then add the beaten egg and a spoonful of the flour. Add the rest of the flour, the salt, the bananas (both kinds if using), and finally the baking powder.

3 Pour the mixture into the lined loaf tin and bake in the oven for around 30 minutes. Check after 25 minutes by inserting a skewer – you want it to come out clean. When it's ready, remove from the oven and let it cool in the tin a little. Then remove and cool completely on a wire rack.

Scones

Is it scone to rhyme with John, or scone to rhyme with Joan? I'm the former, as are most people. However, the 'Joans' do exist. Then there's the whole jam on first or cream on first issue. One is apparently the Devonshire way, the other the Cornish way. It's amazing how uptight people can get about this simple bready cake.

INGREDIENTS
- 250g of self-raising flour
- ½ teaspoon of baking powder
- 50g of cold unsalted butter cut into cubes
- 40g of caster sugar
- 1 egg, beaten
- 70ml of full fat milk

Here's how I like to eat mine. Firstly I take my scone (to rhyme with John) and apply a thin layer of unsalted butter. On to this I spread a good teaspoon of proper clotted cream, and then on top a blob of my home-made damson jam. You see, the jam is slightly sharp, not cloyingly sweet like most commercially-made strawberry jams; my way, the jam hits your taste buds first, then you get the cooling effect from the cream, and the mouth-filling still-warm-from-the-oven taste of the cake. Now that, gents, is how you eat a scone. What's more, they're best eaten the day you make them. You can no more keep a scone in the bread bin than you can keep a kiss there.

The key to making a good scone is not to overwork the dough. Also, they should be a good size. Use a big cutter (7.5cm/3in) – I'm no fan of the small scone. Finally, remember that you can make these savoury too, by adding a little grated cheese.

METHOD

1 Preheat the oven to 200°C. Line a baking tray with baking parchment.
2 Place the flour in a bowl and add the baking powder. Add the butter and rub in until it resembles breadcrumbs. Flour your bench ready for kneading and cutting.
3 In another bowl, beat the egg and add the milk to it. Pour three-quarters of this into the flour mix and combine gently with a palette knife or cutlery knife, rather than your hands. If the dough is too dry, add a bit more of the eggy milk mixture. You want it quite wet.
4 Turn out on to the floured bench and very gently press together. Roll out the dough to a thickness of around 4cm, turning over once or twice as you do so.
5 Using a 7.5cm/3in cutter, cut out your scones. Once you've pressed the cutter firmly into the dough don't twist it as you pull it out, as this can make your scones lean over as they cook. Rather just pull the cutter up and then gently push the scone out of the cutter and on to the waiting baking tray. Don't place them too close together as they'll expand slightly when cooking.
6 Add a drop more milk to the bowl you had the egg and milk in and use that to brush the tops of each scone.
7 Get them in the oven and bake for 15–20 minutes until risen and golden brown. Cool on a wire rack, and then serve.

Optional topping

Jam, cream, cream, jam. Well if you're looking for something a little more adventurous, try the old Cornish variation called 'thunder and lightning', which uses clotted cream and black treacle.

Tea bread

A good tea bread should be as heavy as a house brick. It's one of the cake world's big hitters. This is real 'fill you up' stuff – we're not in the realm of the dainty light-as-a-feather patisserie here. Every cake has its place, and a cake like this is best enjoyed with a steaming cuppa after a yomp through the wilds. It's perhaps no surprise, then, that cakes like this are most popular in places like Yorkshire.

INGREDIENTS

- 250ml of cold black tea made with two teabags
- 200g of mixed fruit
- 100g of raisins
- 50g of chopped dates
- 250g of self-raising flour
- ½ teaspoon of baking powder
- 100g of soft brown sugar
- ½ teaspoon of salt
- ½ teaspoon of cinnamon
- ½ teaspoon of ground ginger
- 1 teaspoon of mixed spice
- 2 eggs, beaten

Tea bread is a dark, heavy, rich fruit cake that calls for the fruits to be soaked overnight in tea. Unlike many other cakes, which can be lovely fresh from the oven, tea bread is best left to settle for a few days in a tin after coming out of the oven, to concentrate the flavour. Like malt loaf, it's great spread with real butter. You could even top it with a slice of Wensleydale cheese for the full Yorkshire experience, by gum.

METHOD

1 Put the teabags in a bowl and pour boiling water from the kettle over them. Add the fruits and leave to soak overnight. In the morning, remove the tea bags.
2 Preheat the oven to 160°C. Grease and line a 2lb/900g loaf tin with baking parchment.
3 Put the flour, baking powder, salt and spices in a bowl. Add the eggs and the stewed fruits plus any remaining liquid.
4 Combine quickly with a spoon and pour into the loaf tin. Bake for 50–60 minutes until firm and a rich dark brown.

Coffee and walnut cake

Apparently a slice of coffee and walnut cake and cup of tea would feature in Nigel Slater's last meal on earth (mine's ham, egg and chips, by the way). To me it's a sort of retro cake, a Victoria sponge after dark. It's the cake the Nescafé Gold Blend couple might enjoy. Indeed, despite coffee being in Britain for centuries this particular combination seems to have achieved its place in the pantheon of British cakes only recently, after instant coffee became available.

INGREDIENTS
For the cake
- 220g of butter
- 220g of golden caster sugar
- 220g of self-raising flour
- 4 medium eggs
- ½ teaspoon of baking powder
- 20ml of strong-brewed espresso coffee
- 70g of finely chopped walnuts plus 12 for decorating

For the buttercream topping
- 125g of unsalted butter
- 200g of icing sugar
- 50ml strong espresso coffee

If you look at some of the older recipes there's not actually any coffee in it, but rather Camp coffee extract, which is made from chicory. Such cakes were more coffee in colour, whereas today I think we want coffee flavour as well. To be honest, I want something that's almost a British tiramisu, a slice of cake that's going to give you a little buzz rather than just a sugary hit. If that's not your thing use instant coffee, which will be a bit weaker in flavour. Needless to say, this isn't really a cake for nippers.

METHOD

1 Preheat the oven to 160°C. Brew the coffee in a stovetop espresso maker or a cafetiere using around 100ml of water. Pour out into a cup and leave to cool. In a small dry frying pan toast the chopped nuts a little to bring out their flavour.

2 Line and grease two 20cm cake tins with baking parchment.

3 In a stand mixer beat the sugar and butter until light and fluffy. Add the eggs one at a time, only adding the next one when the previous one has been fully incorporated. Add the coffee, then add the flour gently and combine.

4 Transfer equally to the cake tins and bake in the middle of the oven for around 25–30 minutes (check after 20). When cooked, turn out on to a wire rack and leave to cool completely.

5 To make the topping, beat the butter and sugar together in a bowl or use a stand mixer, and add the cold coffee. Take one of your cakes and spread a third of the topping over it (if the top of it is too dome-like, level it off with a bread knife). Place the second cake on top and spread the rest of the buttercream over the top of that cake. Arrange the walnut pieces on top spaced equally.

Christmas cake

Every year, on stir-up Sunday (the last Sunday before Advent), I make a Christmas cake. Then over the coming few weeks, I gently inject it with half a bottle of brandy. The first slice is cut on Christmas Eve, and it's often still kicking about in the pantry well into late February. The reason I prefer a Christmas cake rather than a Christmas pudding is precisely this – its longevity. What's more, Christmas cake can take a spread of butter, or even a piece of cheese, as I'm a big fan of Stilton on Christmas cake.

INGREDIENTS

- 500g of mixed fruit
- 500g of raisins (or 300g raisins, 100g cranberries, 100g chopped figs – any dark dried fruits will work)
- Zest and juice of a large orange
- 100ml of brandy (feed the rest to it over Advent)
- 100g of chopped nuts
- 225g of plain flour
- 225g of butter, softened and cut into cubes
- ½ teaspoon of baking powder
- 225g of soft brown sugar
- 2 teaspoons of mixed spice
- 1 teaspoon of ground cinnamon
- ½ teaspoon of ground ginger
- 4 eggs, beaten

METHOD

1 The night before, put the fruit, brandy, zest and juice of the orange in a large bowl and leave overnight to soak.

2 Preheat the oven to 150°C.

3 Belt and braces are needed in the lining department with a long, slow-cooked cake like this. So line the sides and the bottom of a 20cm cake tin with baking parchment and grease well.

4 As an extra precaution, tie a piece of newspaper around the outside of the tin, and have it come up 5–7cm taller than the tin. This will help protect the cake during cooking.

5 Blend the butter and sugar together a little until soft, then add everything else. Stir well until fully combined and there's no pockets of flour or ingredients clumped together – good elbow workout, this. Pour into your lined tin and smooth over with a spatula. Make a slight dip in the centre – this will help ensure a flat top as the cake rises, rather than any dome forming.

6 Bake in a cool to moderate oven for about 2½ hours. Check with a skewer after then. Cool in the tin before turning out on a wire rack and allowing to cool completely.

7 Wrap in cling film and place inside a tin. Every few days, prick the top with a cocktail stick, or better still invest in a flavour injector (like a giant hypodermic needle), and inject it with the rest of the brandy.

8 Cut the first slice on Christmas Day after Her Maj has told you about her year.

Icing on the cake

Traditionally Christmas cakes would be swaddled in layers of marzipan and royal icing (held in place with jam). You can buy both of these ingredients ready-made in shops these days, in which case it's just a roll out, adhere, and coat job. However, here's how to make your own.

INGREDIENTS

For the marzipan
- 200g of brown sugar
- 200g of icing sugar
- 400g of ground almonds
- 2 eggs
- A splash of brandy
- 1–2 drops of vanilla extract or lemon essence
- Pot of jam (apricot is favourite)

For the royal icing
- 250g of icing sugar
- 2 egg whites
- 1 tablespoon of lemon juice

You can buy pretty decent marzipan ready-made, but don't buy the very cheap stuff, as it's tooth-rottingly sweet and tastes of nothing except a faint whiff of disinfectant. Marzipan should be sweet but almondy. And a bit of brandy never hurts.

METHOD

Making the marzipan
1 Put the brown sugar, icing sugar and ground almonds into a bowl or stand mixer.
2 Beat the eggs and mix them in.
3 Add a splash of brandy and a drop or two of vanilla extract or lemon essence.
4 Beat until it's a solid dough. If it's too dry, add more brandy, if it's too wet, some more ground almonds.
5 Place on a board lightly dusted with icing sugar and roll into a flat sheet.
6 Cut a circle 1cm wider than your cake (you can use a plate as a guide).

7 Spread the jam on the top of the cake in a thin layer.
8 Carefully place the marzipan on top.
9 Brush the sides of the cake with jam.
10 Re-roll the rest of the marzipan into long strips and cut so they fit round the edge of your cake. Using more than one strip is fine – just line them up correctly
11 Crimp the top and the edge pieces together.
12 Leave somewhere cool for a day or two to set.

Making the royal icing
1 Beat the lemon juice and egg whites together.
2 Add the sugar and continue beating until fully combined.
3 Royal icing sets hard quickly, so working as fast as you can, apply to the marzipan with a palette knife.

Dorset apple cake

Dorset apple cake, Devon apple cake, Somerset apple cake – each of these West Country counties has its own version, and there's not a huge amount of difference between them to be honest, other than county pride. The Somerset version features some spice including cinnamon and nutmeg, whereas the Devon comes topped with flaked almonds. Oh, and just to not feel left out there's Cornish apple cake too, and even Kent on the other side of the country muscles in on the party.

INGREDIENTS
- 400g of Bramley apples
- Zest and juice of 1 lemon
- 220g of unsalted butter, softened, plus extra for greasing
- 220g of caster sugar
- 4 eggs, beaten
- 220g of self-raising flour
- 2 teaspoons of baking powder
- 30g of ground almonds
- 1 tablespoon of demerara or brown sugar

But no matter what the county, this recipe is really all about celebrating the apple. You'll need cooking apples for this – Bramleys are the most widely available. Indeed, it's ironic with all this county pride that most dessert apples in the shops aren't even from the UK. China is now the world's largest apple (and pretty much everything else) grower, while the UK ranks a lowly 38th. The Bramley, however, is a uniquely British apple, though oddly there's a Bramley apple fan club in Japan.

METHOD

1 Preheat the oven to 160°C and grease and line a 23cm cake tin.
2 Peel and core the apples then dice into small chunks. Squeeze the lemon over the top of them and coat thoroughly. This will stop them discolouring too much.
3 In a stand mixer or bowl, beat together the butter, sugar and lemon zest until light and fluffy. Add one of the beaten eggs, then a large spoonful of the flour, then repeat for the other three eggs. Add the rest of the flour.
4 Add the baking powder and combine, then add the ground almonds and the pieces of apple.
5 Spoon into the baking tin and smooth down the surface with a spatula or palette knife. Sprinkle over the brown sugar – this will melt as it cooks to give a little crunch.
6 Bake for 1 hour and then check with a skewer. It might need another few minutes.
7 Leave in the tin to cool for 10 minutes before turning out on to a wire rack. Dust with a little more icing sugar and leave to cool completely.
8 Serve with clotted cream.

Lemon drizzle cake

Lemon drizzle is one of those cakes that, when done well, is almost refreshing. When done badly it's like eating the sugar bowl. Sugar should be present as part of a light frosting, not piled up like a snowdrift.

INGREDIENTS

For the cake
- 220g of unsalted butter at room temperature
- 220g of caster sugar
- 4 eggs (should weigh around 220g)
- 220g of plain flour
- Zest of a well-washed lemon
- Tablespoon of chopped candied lemon peel
- 3 teaspoons of baking powder

For the lemon drizzle
- 80g of caster sugar
- Juice of two lemons

I've dialled up the lemon factor by including candied lemon peel, which you can find in most bakery sections of supermarkets. Finally, I like to make this in a loaf tin, but use a round one if you prefer. You can even make individual ones in mini loaf tins.

METHOD

1 Preheat the oven to 170°C. Grease and line a loaf tin. Zest your lemon and assemble other ingredients.
2 Place butter and sugar in the bowl of your stand mixer and attach the creaming or K-beater attachment. Cream together until light and fluffy.
3 Add the flour, the lemon zest, the candied lemon peel if using and lastly the baking powder and combine.
4 Transfer the mixture to your tin and smooth over with a spatula or palette knife.
5 Place in the oven and bake for around 20–25 minutes. Test with a metal skewer, and if it comes out clean it's done.
6 Leave to cool for 5 minutes before removing from the tin and gently peeling off the baking parchment.
7 Place a wire rack over a sheet of newspaper and place the cake on it. Using a cocktail stick prick the top of the cake all over.
8 Make the glaze by mixing the sugar with the lemon juice. You want the sugar to dissolve, so give it a good stir.
9 Drizzle the lemon drizzle over the cake and leave to cool.

Parkin

Parkin is little known outside the counties of Yorkshire or Lancashire, which, like some cake-themed War of the Roses, each have slightly different variations. Yorkshire parkin often features lard as well as coarsely ground oats, whereas Lancashire parkin uses finer milled oats, resulting in a closer texture.

INGREDIENTS

- 100g of porridge oats
- 220g of self-raising flour
- 1 pinch of salt
- 100g of softened unsalted butter
- 50g of lard
- 100g of dark muscovado sugar
- 70g of black treacle
- 170g of golden syrup
- 1 teaspoon of baking powder
- 1 teaspoon of ground ginger
- 1 teaspoon of ground nutmeg
- 3 teaspoons of mixed spice
- 2 medium eggs, beaten
- 2 tablespoons of milk

Parkin improves if you give it a few days to itself in a tin, where it slowly mellows and grows sticky, after which it's ready to set your Bonfire Night off with a bang.

METHOD

1 Preheat oven to 140°C.
2 Lightly grease a 20cm x 20cm square cake tin with a neutral oil or a little butter.
3 In a pan, gently melt the butter, lard, sugar, treacle and golden syrup. Don't let it bubble.
4 In a large mixing bowl, combine the flour, oats, salt and spices. Gradually add the melted sugar mixture and combine, then add the eggs and milk.
5 Pour into the greased baking tin and bake for around 1 hour. Check to see how it's doing and continue to bake for another 20 minutes. You want it firm and set.
6 When it's baked, remove and leave to cool on a wire rack before wrapping in cling film or greaseproof paper and storing in a tin for a few days.

A history of parkin

Parkin. The mere word sounds as comforting as a hot toddy on a drizzly November night. It's a fitting name for a cake that's both fiery and sweet, and just the thing to reach for when the nights draw in and winter announces its arrival. Over 1,500 years ago the Vikings celebrated this time of year with cakes made from oats and honey baked on a hot stone. These simple hotcakes are likely to be the more sober ancestors to the deeply spicy, gingery, sticky cake that we now know as parkin.

The rather less pagan Victorians kept the cake, if not the sentiment, and made parkin for their Bonfire Night festivities. It's an apt association, as a good parkin should have something of the snap of gunpowder about it in taste, and be as squidgy as Semtex.

The primary ingredient is still oats, which grow well in the cool north of Britain. Nearly all the other ingredients are products of the Victorian era, however, and come from an empire far greater than the Vikings could ever have imagined.

Raw cane sugar from the West Indies was refined in London, and the by-products made into treacle and golden syrup, which add sweetness and stickiness and, in the case of treacle, a dark, rich colour. The cake's unmistakable warmth comes from a key ingredient, ginger. It and other spices that are sometimes added to parkin, such as nutmeg, cinnamon and mace, were all brought to Britain from the spice markets of the Middle East and Asia.

Parkin was so admired in the North in the Victorian era that the first Sunday of November was known as Parkin Sunday in the West Riding of Yorkshire, and Mary Gaskill's *A Yorkshire Cookery Book* of 1917 gives recipes for 17 different versions.

The key to a good parkin is using dark muscovado sugar, which gives an almost nutty flavour. This, along with a bit of black treacle and golden syrup, ensures the sticky consistency that lifts parkin from a mere ginger-flavoured cake into something special.

In her 1950 book *Traditional Recipes of the British Isles*, Nell Heaton advises a glass of warm milk to be served with parkin for children on Bonfire Night.

Chocolate cake

Chocolate and cake. Need I say more? All too often many chocolate cakes are just Victoria sponges made brown by the addition of cocoa powder, but not this one. Also, it's one single cake, which means you don't have to think about a filling. Finally, the ganache coating gives extra moistness and more chocolate flavour. Enjoy.

INGREDIENTS

For the cake
- 100ml of full fat milk (at room temperature, or warm a little in the microwave)
- 250g of unsalted butter cut into cubes, plus extra for greasing
- 200g of 70–80% dark chocolate
- 250g of plain flour
- 60g of cocoa powder
- 250g of caster sugar
- 4 teaspoons of baking powder
- 5 eggs, beaten
- 1 teaspoon of vanilla extract
- 50ml of water
- 50ml of vegetable oil

For the ganache coating
- 225ml of double cream
- 350g of broken-up plain chocolate

METHOD

1 Preheat oven to 140°C.
2 Grease and line a deep 23cm springform cake tin.
3 Sieve a glass bowl over a pan of barely simmering water and add the milk, butter and chocolate. Gently heat until thoroughly melted and combined.
4 Place the flour into a bowl and add the cocoa powder, the sugar and the baking powder.
5 Fold in the chocolate mixture, the eggs, the vanilla extract, the water and the oil, and fold gently together until combined.
6 Pour into the cake tin and shake a little to even out the batter.
7 Place in the oven and bake for 60–75 minutes. Check with a skewer – it should come out of the cake clean.
8 Leave in the tin on a wire rack to cool.
9 Wash and dry the bowl you melted the chocolate in. Add the cream and the broken-up chocolate and heat gently until fully combined. Leave to cool and when set use a palette knife to apply to the sides and the top of the cake in a coating.

Depending on how thick you like your ganache, you might end up with some left over. Don't waste it – place it in the fridge to set and then, using a teaspoon (a melon baller would be better, but who's got one of those? Not me), scoop out a good chunk. Roll into a ball quickly using your hands and dust in a little cocoa powder. You've now got chocolate truffles. You can eat these separately, or use them to decorate the top of the cake.

Orange and saffron cake

Now, I'm a firm believer in recipe ingredients that are all available from your average local shop – not for me the obscure things you have to order online or seek out in health food shops. However, in this case I'll make an exception, because it calls for a tiny pinch of English saffron as well as a measure of King Harry orange and saffron liqueur. This stunning alcoholic drink is made with gin from Cambridge, infused with saffron and real oranges. It has a gorgeous orange colour and bright zesty flavour, and is available from www.norfolksaffron. co.uk. It's one for the drinks cabinet, as it also makes a wicked sidecar cocktail.

INGREDIENTS

- 2 large oranges (navel ones are good as they have no pips; if you're using others, remove pips before blitzing)
- 6 eggs
- 1 tablespoon of King Harry orange and saffron liqueur
- 3 strands of English saffron
- 250g of caster sugar
- 300g of ground almonds
- 1 teaspoon of baking powder
- Knob of butter for greasing
- Teaspoon of flour for flouring the tin

For the orange syrup

- 300ml of orange juice
- 100g of caster sugar

Incidentally, it was the legendary Claudia Roden who switched British cake fans on to this style of boiled orange cake with a recipe that first appeared in *A Book of Middle Eastern Food* in 1968. Back then no one had a food processor, and the boiled oranges had to be rubbed through a sieve by hand!

METHOD

1 Place the whole oranges in a pan of water and gently boil for 2 hours – top up the water if it needs it.

2 Remove and when cool enough to handle cut into quarters and place in a food processor. Add the saffron and the orange liqueur too. Blitz to a smooth paste and allow to cool completely (this can take an hour, so feel free to do this bit in advance).

3 Preheat the oven to 160°C.

4 Grease a 23cm cake tin with butter, then sieve in the flour and shake around so it sticks to the butter.

5 In a stand mixer or a large mixing bowl, beat the eggs together, add the cooled orange pulp and the rest of the ingredients and mix thoroughly.

6 Pour into the greased and floured tin and bake in the oven for around an hour. Check with a skewer to see if it's done – it should come out clean. If not, give it a little longer.

7 Leave to cool in the tin before removing.

8 To make the syrup, place the orange juice and sugar in a pan over a medium heat until the sugar has dissolved. Turn down to a simmer and reduce until the sauce is a syrup-like consistency.

9 Cut the cake into wedges and serve with the syrup. You can garnish with more thinly sliced orange if you like. A squeeze of honey would be a good alternative if you don't want to make the syrup.

Pear upside down cake

I've gone for pears rather than the traditional pineapple in this classic retro recipe. Other fruits, both tinned and fresh, are also fair game, such as apricots or even blueberries. You can pretty much upside-downificate anything.

I'd be wary about using a springform tin with a removable base for this recipe, as you might get a bit of liquid leakage. If you've not got a solid tin, just put a baking tray or dish underneath. Alternatively you could make it in a loaf tin – reduce the amounts a little, though.

INGREDIENTS

- 4 tablespoons of golden syrup
- 1 can of pear halves in syrup (410g)
- 100g of butter, plus extra for greasing
- 100g of caster sugar
- 2 eggs, beaten
- 150g of plain flour
- 2 teaspoons of baking powder
- 1 teaspoon of vanilla extract
- A little milk

METHOD

1 Preheat the oven to 180°C.
2 Open and drain the pears and measure out the other ingredients.
3 Grease a 20cm cake tin with butter. Heat the golden syrup in a pan or jug in the microwave and pour into the cake tin. Arrange the pears in a circle around the tin, with one in the centre.
4 Cream the butter and sugar together by hand or in a stand mixer until light and fluffy.
5 Add the beaten egg, vanilla extract and flour and combine. Lastly, add the baking powder. You want a dropping consistency – if the mixture's a little thick, thin with a drop or two of milk.
6 Spread over the fruit and smooth down with a palette knife.
7 Cook in the oven for about 45 minutes (check with a skewer after 40) until the sponge is risen and golden. Allow to cool in the tin a little, and turn out on to a serving plate so the fruit is at the top.
8 Serve with custard or cream or reduce the syrup the pears came in in a pan and pour over.

Beetroot cake

I'll fess up, I'm not beetroot's biggest fan. Growing up there was only the pickled variety, which puckered my young mouth. Beetroots are earthy, wholesome and, let's face it, a little bit boring. Combine them with chocolate, however, and things get much more fun.

INGREDIENTS
- 250g pack of cooked beetroot
- 200g of good quality dark chocolate (min 70% cocoa)
- 200g of plain flour
- 3 teaspoons of baking powder
- 200g of unsalted butter, melted
- 150g of caster sugar
- 4 eggs
- 2 tablespoons of cocoa powder

Unlike the veg in carrot cake, beetroots don't really bring any sweetness to the mix; instead they bring colour and that deep earthy flavour that works so well with good, dark chocolate.

You can buy fresh beetroots and roast them whole in the oven, then scoop out the flesh, or even grate raw beetroot into the cake mix. The downside with this is that you'll probably end up with your fingers stained pink. It's far easier to buy them ready-cooked in a packet. Some supermarkets even do ones with extra flavours, like chilli, which would make an interesting additional flavour. Or you could add a pinch of chilli powder.

METHOD
1 Preheat the oven to 160°C.
2 Grease and line a round cake tin.
3 A food processor renders making this cake much easier.
4 Melt the butter in a pan or the microwave. Break the chocolate into small chunks.
5 Cut the beetroot in half and blitz in the food processor. Add the eggs one at a time and briefly blitz after each. Then add the melted butter and the chocolate pieces. Give it a final blitz.
6 Put the flour, baking powder, cocoa powder and sugar in a bowl. Add the wet chocolate beetroot mix and fully combine (if your food processor's big enough you can do this in it).
7 Tip into the cake tin and smooth over the top with a palette knife.
8 Bake in the oven for 40–45 minutes until a cake skewer comes out clean.
9 Leave to cool for a few minutes then remove from the tin and dust with icing sugar.
10 Serve as is, or with a little *crème fraîche*.

Carrot cake

The story often goes that carrot cake was 'invented' during World War Two to sweeten cakes, as sugar was rationed. In fact it was more likely *rediscovered*, since carrots have been used in cakes and puddings for centuries. Hannah Glasse's famous cookbook from 1747 contains a recipe for carrot pudding. But there's examples even older than that – one medieval Middle Eastern cookbook also has a carrot pudding, along with a carrot drink and carrot-based medicine.

INGREDIENTS

For the cake
- 250g of self-raising flour
- Teaspoon of cinnamon
- ½ a freshly ground nutmeg
- 1 teaspoon of bicarbonate of soda
- 185g of soft brown sugar
- 60g of chopped pecans or walnuts
- 3 tablespoons of honey
- 300g of grated carrots
- 225ml of vegetable oil
- 4 eggs, beaten

For the icing
- 2 tablespoons of orange juice
- 200g of full fat cream cheese
- 60g of unsalted butter, softened
- 170g of icing sugar

Of course, today a bag of sugar probably costs less than a bag of carrots, but we still love our carrot cake. Modern carrot cakes aren't exactly shining examples of austerity either, as most are packed with nuts and topped with sugary frosting. But you know, it's *kind of* one of your five a day...

METHOD

1 Preheat the oven to 160°C.
2 Lightly grease a 23cm cake tin and line with baking parchment.
3 Sift the flour, the spice and the bicarbonate of soda into a large bowl, add the sugar, the honey, the nuts and the carrots and combine. Make a well in the centre and stir in the beaten egg and the vegetable oil.
4 Spoon into the baking tin and smooth down the surface with a spatula or palette knife.
5 Bake for 1 hour and then check with a skewer – it might need another few minutes.
6 Leave in the tin to cool for 10 minutes before turning out on to a wire rack. Leave to cool completely.
7 To make the icing, beat the butter and cream cheese together in a stand mixer or using a wooden spoon. Gradually add the icing sugar, and slacken with a little of the orange juice. You want something light, creamy and spreadable.
8 Using a palette knife spread over the top of the cooled cake, and grate over a little orange zest or chopped walnuts.

CHAPTER 5
BISCUITS, SWEETS, BUNS AND SMALL CAKES

I'm not sure why, but it feels OK to eat a biscuit mid-morning, whereas cake feels distinctly an afternoon thing. Perhaps it's because it's so soon after breakfast. Indeed, it's items like this that are great for taking into work. Biscuits, cookies, flapjacks and their kin are great to munch with a mid-morning cuppa. Dairy doesn't feature in most of these recipes, which means they'll have a long shelf life if kept cool in an airtight container.

Shortbread

The monarch of the glen as far as Scottish baking goes, and found on tea-trays in B&Bs and hotel conference suites all over the UK. They're also really easy to make. As butter is key to a good shortbread, buy a really good-quality one. The end result should be a crumbly, sweetish biscuit that gives a warm buttery finish in the mouth.

INGREDIENTS

- 220g of plain flour
- 190g of butter
- 70g of caster sugar
- Pinch of salt

METHOD

1 Place the butter and flour in a food processor and blitz until it resembles fine breadcrumbs. Add the sugar and blitz again until fully combined.

2 Turn out on to a lightly floured work surface and, working quickly, roll out to just over 1cm thick.

3 Using a cutter cut into shapes, either individual circles or long fingers. If you want to make petticoat tails, place a saucer on the dough and cut round it, or use a very large cutter or ring. Then, using a ruler, make six light indentations in a star formation on the surface of the dough.

4 Sprinkle with caster sugar and place in the fridge for 20 minutes to firm up.

5 Bake in a cool oven at 150°C for 20–25 minutes until light golden brown. The smaller the biscuit, the quicker it will cook. Set aside to cool.

Millionaire's shortbread

No one is exactly sure how millionaire's shortbread got its name. The *Oxford English Dictionary* says it was known in Scotland from the early 1990s. It's certainly nothing to do with the ingredients being expensive (flour, butter, chocolate and condensed milk hardly require a trip to a Swiss bank), or to them being 'rich' in taste compared to any other recipe in this book.

INGREDIENTS

For the shortbread
- 220g of plain flour
- 190g of butter
- 70g of caster sugar
- Pinch of salt

For the caramel filling
- 170g of butter
- 1 small tin can (379g) of condensed milk
- 3 tablespoons of golden syrup

For the chocolate topping
- 300g of dark chocolate, melted

Nor can it be historic in origin, featuring as it does, tins of condensed milk. A bake featuring exactly the same ingredients appeared in an Australian magazine in the late 1970s, where it went by the name chocolate caramel squares.

METHOD

1 Preheat oven to 150°C.

2 Line a 23cm square tin with two sheets of baking parchment, one running top to bottom and the other left to right. You want the paper to extend over the edges of the tin – this will help in lifting the finished bake out. Grease lightly with butter.

3 Place the butter and flour in a food processor and blitz until it resembles fine breadcrumbs. Alternatively rub in by hand (page 41).

4 Add the sugar and blitz until fully combined, then transfer to your cake tin. Press down firmly – if you've got another cake tin exactly the same size use that rather than your hands, as it will create even pressure. If not, start with your hands and then try and use something else flat to ensure the mix is level. You want it tightly packed together. Bake in the oven at 150°C for 25–30 minutes until light golden brown. Set aside to cool (this can be done the day before if you like).

5 While that's cooking make the caramel. Gently melt the butter in a pan and add the condensed milk and golden syrup. Increase the heat a little and stir regularly to ensure it doesn't stick on the bottom of the pan. It'll start to boil and turn a golden-brown toffee colour. When is does let it cool a little before pouring it over the cooked shortbread. Move the tin around to ensure even distribution. Let it cool completely.

6 Melt the chocolate in a microwave or in a bowl over a saucepan of barely simmering water until completely liquid. Pour over the cool caramel and leave to set in the fridge. You don't want too much chocolate on top as this will set much harder than the caramel underneath, meaning when you bite into it it pushes down and pushes the caramel filling out the sides. Try and aim for something like 3–5mm. Cut into squares and serve with a cuppa.

Hot-cross or not crossed buns

Like much of baking, home-made hot-cross buns take some beating. I also think these buns are too good just to eat during Easter, which was when they were traditionally made and eaten – they're great around autumn-time too. Don't skimp on the spices, though, otherwise you'll be left with a bread roll.

INGREDIENTS

- 350ml of warm milk
- 100g of unsalted butter
- 12g of instant fast action yeast
- 80g of caster sugar
- 1 teaspoon of salt
- 600g of strong white flour
- 20g of wholemeal flour
- 2 teaspoons of mixed spice
- 1 teaspoon of ground cinnamon
- 1 teaspoon of ground nutmeg
- 2 eggs, beaten
- 250g of mixed fruits
- 3 tablespoons of apricot jam or marmalade to glaze
- 50g of plain flour for the cross (if using – see points 8 and 9)

METHOD

1 Put the milk in a saucepan and bring up to the boil, then turn out the heat. Add the butter to the milk to melt.

2 In a bowl combine the yeast, flours, sugar, spices, fruit and salt. Make a well in the middle and add the milk and melted butter, slowly mixing together to combine.

3 Knead for five minutes until the dough is elastic.

4 Place in an oiled bowl, cover with cling film and leave to prove for 1 hour or until it's doubled in size.

5 Knock the dough back and transfer to your work surface. Knead for a minute or two then divide into 16 equal-sized portions. Check these by weighing them – ideally you want them all the same size.

6 Place on an oiled baking tray at least 3–4cm apart, dust with a little flour, cover with a clean tea towel or oil cling film and leave for 30–45 minutes.

7 Preheat the oven to 180°C.

8 Now, I don't often bother with a cross – I don't think it adds anything flavour-wise, and it's only there for symbolic reasons. Sometimes I do a swirl or other pattern instead, which is how they become 'not crossed buns'. But if you want to keep things traditional, do the following.

9 Mix the flour with a little water until you've got a paste. Place in a piping bag and slowly pipe the flour mixture over the buns in a cross shape.

10 Place in the oven and bake for around 20 minutes until golden brown.

11 While they're baking, prepare the glaze, warm the jam in the microwave and pick out any big lumps with a teaspoon.

12 When the buns come out of the oven let them cool for a few minutes before applying the glaze with a pastry brush.

Fat rascals

Fat rascals are now chiefly associated with Yorkshire and its most famous tearoom chain, Bettys (yes, no apostrophe). Bettys developed the current version, featuring two glacé cherry 'eyes' above a mouth made of almonds, in 1983, and it's since gone on to become their bestseller, so much so that they've even trademarked it. They now sell over 375,000 fat rascals per year.

INGREDIENTS
Makes 4–6

For the buns
- 250g of plain flour
- 100g of butter (at room temperature)
- 70g of golden caster sugar
- Pinch of sea salt
- 100g of mixed dried fruits
- 1½ teaspoons of baking powder
- Zest of an orange
- Zest of a lemon
- 1 egg, beaten
- A splash of milk to loosen the dough a little

For the decoration and glaze
- 1 egg yolk
- Teaspoon of water
- Flaked or whole almonds
- Glacé cherries

They're a sort of cross between a bun, a scone and a rock cake, quite firm and raised using bicarbonate of soda or baking powder. Historical versions would have been cooked in a pan with a lid over a peat turf fire, rather than an oven.

The name is an interesting one. A rascal is a very old term once used to describe an undersized, scrawny or young stag. So a 'fat' rascal is an oxymoron. Shakespeare uses the term 'fat rascal' in *Henry IV Part II*. The phrase is first used to describe a generic small tea cake in Yorkshire in 1855.

METHOD

1 Preheat the oven to 190°C and have a non-stick baking tin ready.
2 Rub in the butter and flour either in a food processor or with your fingers until it resembles breadcrumbs. Add the sugar, dried fruits, salt, zest of orange and lemon and combine. Add the baking powder.
3 Make the glaze, mix a little water (or milk) with the egg yolk and have standing by.
4 Now add the whole egg to the dough mix and bring together, but don't work it too much. If it's really dry, add a splash of milk (about as much as you'd have in your tea). You don't want this too loose.
5 Scoop out a portion the size of a squash ball and gently roll into a ball in your hands. You want a scone-like mix, not too wet and not too overworked. Place on the baking sheet and slightly squash down. Repeat until all your dough is used up.
6 Place the glacé cherry eyes on and make a smile with the almonds. Glaze generously with the egg mix and place in the oven for around 20 minutes until golden brown. Leave to cool before serving.

Gingerbread

What connects Ashbourne, Brighton, Grantham, Grasmere, Ormskirk, Market Drayton, Preston, Sledmere, Wakefield and Whitby? Well, they're just some of the regional variations of gingerbread we have here in Britain. Naturally there's a tall tale behind some of them as to how they came to be – Ashbourne gingerbread was supposedly created by a French prisoner of the Napoleonic wars who settled in Ashbourne.

INGREDIENTS

- 225g of plain flour
- Pinch of salt
- 1 teaspoon of bicarbonate of soda
- 3 teaspoons of ground ginger
- 100g of butter
- 40g of soft brown sugar
- 2 tablespoons of golden syrup
- 1 tablespoon of treacle
- 1 egg, beaten
- 300ml of warm milk

All these cakes come from a time when each region had its own regional variation, something we rarely see in baking these days. The common ingredient, unsurprisingly, is ginger, but after that things differ wildly. Some are small flapjack-like biscuits, others great big sticky brown cakes, some call for almonds, others for oats, and many add treacle, but not all.

METHOD

1 Preheat oven to 170°C.
2 Grease and line the bottom of a square baking tin with baking parchment.
3 Place the flour, salt and ginger in a bowl. Warm the butter, sugar, syrup and treacle in a pan until the butter has melted. Add this to the dry ingredients, then add the milk, the beaten egg and lastly the bicarbonate of soda.
4 Pour into the lined tin and bake for 45 minutes to an hour until a rich golden brown. Test with a skewer. When cooked, leave to cool slightly before turning out on to a wire rack.
5 Slice into fingers. It'll keep wrapped in foil or sealed in a tin – nice with a dollop of cream as a quick pud.

Another variation is a biscuit, usually cut into the shape of a person. The associated story first appeared in a US children's magazine in 1875 (though it may be much older) which sees a gingerbread boy running away from people – 'Run, run as fast as you can! You can't catch me. I'm the Gingerbread Man!' – until, of course, he's eventually eaten by a fox.

Chelsea buns

Chelsea buns are made from an egg-enriched dough, which is rolled out into a flat sheet, then topped with butter, lots of sugar and dried fruits. It's then rolled up and cut into wheels, which are packed snugly in a baking tray. After baking they're glazed with either golden syrup, honey or apricot jam. The result is a coiled sticky bun that you eat by unravelling it.

INGREDIENTS

For the dough
- 500g of strong white bread flour
- 50g of caster sugar
- 7g of fast action yeast
- 1 egg, beaten
- 50g of softened unsalted butter
- 1 teaspoon of salt
- 250ml of warm milk

For the filling
- 30g of butter
- 70g of soft brown sugar
- 2 teaspoons of cinnamon
- 100g of mixed fruit
- 50g of raisins

For the glaze
- Three tablespoons of golden syrup

You need a big, high-sided roasting tray for this, well greased and lined with baking parchment. If you've not got such a tray you can use a flat one, but the buns won't have that distinctive cylindrical shape.

METHOD

1 Sift the flour into a bowl and add the yeast on one side of the bowl and the salt on the other. Melt the 50g of butter for the dough in a pan, add the milk and warm to blood temperature. Add the egg to the flour, mix a little, then add the warm milk and butter.

2 Work together into a dough in the bowl until well combined and the sides of the bowl are clean. Then turn out on to a well-floured surface. Alternatively you can do all of this in a stand mixer. Knead the dough for around five minutes until it's smooth, almost shiny, and no longer sticky.

3 Transfer the dough to a lightly oiled mixing bowl. Cover with cling film and leave to prove for 1 hour. The dough should double in size.

4 While it's proving, line a 34cm x 24cm roasting tin with baking parchment and lightly oil – you don't want to be chipping these out of the tin. Have enough outside the tin so that you can lift the finished buns out.

5 Melt the 30g of butter for the filling (you can use the same pan as before).

6 When the dough is proved transfer back to the bench and roll into a large rectangular shape.

7 Brush the dough with the melted butter, then sprinkle over the sugar, cinnamon and the dried fruits.

8 Take the longest edge of the sheet of dough and gently roll towards the other side.

9 Once rolled, cut into 12 pieces. Do this by cutting in half, then cut each half in half again, then each piece into thirds. Don't press down with the knife – saw gently through instead, as you want to maintain the coil shape.

10 Preheat the oven to 200°C.

11 Place in the tin and leave to prove for around another 30 minutes, by which time they should have swelled up and be nearly touching one another.

12 Bake in the oven for 20–25 minutes, until golden brown and well risen. Lift out of the pan using the paper and place on a wire rack to cool.

13 Meanwhile heat the golden syrup for the glaze in a pan. Brush over the cooling buns with a pastry brush. Tear off each bun and serve with a cuppa.

Buns of Britain

The Bun House in Chelsea in south-west London was established in the late 17th century by Richard Gideon Hand. The Bun House's exact location isn't clear. There's some evidence to point to Jew's Road, now called Pimlico Road. What's more, it seems to have changed name, and in the 1790s became known as the Royal Bun House. This was probably due to the fact that royalty as well as commoners now enjoyed the buns. Indeed, Queen Charlotte presented Mrs Hand with a large silver mug as a gift.

The Scottish writer Thomas Carlyle, who lived at 5 Cheyne Walk, wrote to his mother on 29 March 1850 saying, 'I went out for a walk this morning; all was grey, dim, and snell [harsh] as winter: but at the "Original Chelsea Bunhouse" there was a gathering; I stept near, it was poor souls crowding forward for their buns, and Baker and Wife serving them eagerly out of door and window'. They're as popular now as they were back then, with Jane Grigson declaring them 'the best of all buns, on account of their melting, buttery sweetness' in her book *English Food*.

BAPS, BARMS, BATCH, COBS AND ROLLS

While the name bun is generally applied to sweet round breads in the UK, nomenclature gets complicated for the savoury version depending on where you live. In the North-East they have stotties; the North-West have barm cakes; Yorkshire goes for muffins; Shropshire and the Midlands have batches or cobs; and Liverpool apparently prefers nudgers; while South Wales opts for baps, as do bits of Scotland. Yet despite all these regional variations, everyone knows what you mean when you ask for a roll.

BATH'S BUNS

The city of Bath has been responsible for inventing various buns and biscuits. It's home to the Sally Lunn bun, the Bath bun and finally Bath Olivers. Sally Lunn buns are, according to the Sally Lunn teashop in the town, the creation of one Solange Luyon, a young Huguenot refugee. She secured work in a bakery in town and is said to have created a rich, brioche-style bread, which the people of Bath christened the 'Sally Lunn' bun.

However, there are other theories as to how it got its name. Some think it's a corruption of 'sol et lune' (sun and moon) due to the round, golden sun shape of the crust and the soft, white, moonlike interior.

Bath buns are similar, but often contain caraway seed. These were said to have been invented by Dr William Oliver, who believed in the restorative powers of the city's waters and opened up what we'd now call a 'health farm'. His patients, however, enjoyed his buns rather too much, so he invented the Bath Oliver, made from flour, milk, fresh butter, malt and hops, the world's first diet biscuit.

THE CHELSEA BUN-HOUSE, 1810. (*From Mr. Crace's Collection.*)

Flapjacks

After chocolate rice crispy cakes these are the first thing that many of us learn to make, often while at school. There's something homely and timeless about flapjacks. They're permanently out of fashion, yet if you say 'Fancy a flapjack?' when offering an unexpected house guest a cuppa, folk will always say yes.

INGREDIENTS
- 300g of unsalted butter
- 250g of golden syrup
- 500g of porridge oats

or
- 450g porridge oats and 50g jumbo oats if you like the odd big flake

There's two rival camps in the world of flapjackery: chewy versus crunchy. I am firmly, squarely and proudly in the chewy camp – crunchy is just too much hard work in the mouth. However, up the oven temperature if you like them crunchy. You could also experiment with reducing the golden syrup a bit and using maple syrup.

Finally I also give short shrift to gussied-up flapjacks featuring seeds, berries and other 'healthy' things. A flapjack should be about butter, syrup and oats.

METHOD
1 Preheat oven to 160°C.
2 In a saucepan, melt the butter and add the golden syrup. Add the oats and stir well to combine so that all the oats are covered.
3 Line a square cake tin with baking parchment and spoon the mixture in. Press down firmly. You should have enough mixture to give you a finished flapjack that is over 1cm in height. Bake for 20–25 minutes until golden. Remove and leave to cool for a bit before cutting into rectangles.

Home-made hobnobs

Hobnobs – the body of a flapjack, the shape of a digestive. It's a winning combination perfect for dipping in a brew. It's no wonder that Peter Kay described them as the Marines of the biscuit world. 'Again! Again! Dip me again, I'm going nowhere me, son, dip me! Is that all you've got? Come on!'

INGREDIENTS
- 250g of self-raising flour
- 250g of porridge oats
- 250g of caster sugar
- 250g of unsalted butter
- 1 tablespoon of golden syrup
- 1 tablespoon of water
- ½ teaspoon of bicarbonate of soda

Now, you may be thinking 'Hang on, I can buy a packet of hobnobs for under a quid from the shops. Why would I make them from scratch?' And yes, you can. But making your own is not only pretty easy (if you have young children they'll enjoy it too), it also means you can make giant versions, and who doesn't like jumbo-sized hobnobs?

METHOD
1 Preheat oven to 160°C.
2 Place a sheet of baking parchment on a baking tray. Place another sheet of paper on your bench.
3 Mix the flour, bicarbonate of soda and the oats in a bowl, then melt the butter, golden syrup and caster sugar in a pan. Add to the oats and flour mixture and combine.
4 Tip out the mixture on to the second piece of parchment and press flat using your hands. Dust a rolling pin with flour and roll to a thickness of 1cm.
5 Using a large cutter, or any other shape you like such as people or stars, cut out as many biscuits as you can and place on the lined baking tray. Any trimmings can be quickly brought back together, re-rolled and cut again.
6 Bake in the oven for 15 minutes until cooked. Leave to cool and put the kettle on.

Apple roses

Short on ingredients but big on the wow factor, this recipe does take a bit of skill to put together, but it looks ace if you can pull if off. Just work quickly, but carefully, and keep everything cold and you should be fine. It's just a coil of pastry, similar to a Chelsea bun but with apple slices.

INGREDIENTS

- 2 large red apples
- 1 sheet of pre-made puff pastry
- 1 tablespoon of apricot or other fruit jam
- Tablespoon of melted butter
- Icing sugar for dusting

Ideally you'll need a mandolin to slice the apples. If you've not got one you can use a knife, but remember, you want the slices very thin so they'll bend as you coil up the pastry. Or if you've got a box-shaped cheese grater look on the side – there might be a slicer there you can use.

METHOD

1 Preheat oven to 180°C.
2 First melt the butter and the jam in two small dishes or ramekins in the microwave and set aside.
3 Then slice the apples in half and cut out the cores with your small knife. Slice on a mandolin into semicircles.
4 Take your pastry from the fridge and unfurl. On a lightly dusted surface cut off a strip from the longest side about 6cm in depth. You should get three from the sheet of puff pastry.
5 Lay the apple pieces, peel-side up, along the top half slightly, over the edge, and brush the bottom half with the warm jam.
6 Fold up the bottom half to hold the apple slices in place and then roll the whole strip from left to right into a tight coil. You should have a petal-like arrangement. Tease open the ones nearest the edge.
7 Use the butter to grease a muffin tray and place each flower in it.
8 Brush with a little more melted butter, just to get a bit of colour in the oven. You can chill them back in the fridge at this point and bake when ready. In fact that would be a good thing.
9 Place in the oven and bake for 10–15 minutes until the pastry has cooked.
10 Remove from the tin and dust with a little icing sugar once cooled.

Profiteroles

In the 16th century 'prophytrolles', as they were then known, were savoury dumplings served with soups, stews and fish, and were cooked in the ashes of the fire. The modern version, made from choux pastry and filled with cream, is only known from the late 19th century. On reflection I think we get the better deal.

INGREDIENTS

For the pastry
- 250ml water
- 100g unsalted butter
- 150g plain flour
- 3 eggs
- Teaspoon of salt and sugar

For the filling and the coating
- 300ml of whipping cream
- 150g of milk chocolate

Note: choux pastry doesn't always have to be sweet – you can make savoury dishes too. Replace half the water with milk in the recipe above and add a strong cheese after you've incorporated the eggs and you have gougères, which are great with drinks.

The traditional way to serve them is arranged in a pyramid and topped with chocolate sauce. The French, of course, take this one step further in the dish Croquembouche (pictured below), which translates as something which crunches in the mouth. It's a giant cone of choux pastry balls held together with lots of caramel. They're often served as the finale to ceremonies such as weddings, baptisms and communions.

Most recipes say use a piping bag to make the balls on the tray, but you can also use two teaspoons. Remember, they're going to puff up and more than double in size, so you only want balls about the size of a walnut.

METHOD

1 Preheat the oven to 200°C.
2 Prepare your equipment. Fit the nozzle to the piping bag and grease two large baking trays with vegetable oil.
3 Place the butter and water in a pan and heat until the butter has melted. Bring up to a rolling boil then remove from the heat on to a firm surface.
4 Add the flour to the pan and beat into the liquid with a wooden spoon.
5 Continue beating until the mixture doesn't stick to the side of the pan and forms a ball. There should be no clumps of flour remaining.
6 Leave until cool enough to handle, then give the pastry a final beating to release any remaining heat.
7 Add the beaten eggs a bit at a time, making sure you incorporate fully before adding the next bit. Your dough should be shiny and drop off the spoon reluctantly.
8 Transfer to your piping bag and pipe little blobs about the size of a walnut on to both of the trays, leaving room for them to expand. Press down on to the tray with the end of the nozzle to break off the dough into the right amounts. If you've not got a piping bag, you can try making small balls of dough using two teaspoons.
9 Bake in the oven for 5–10 minutes before reducing the temperature to 160°C and baking for a further 5 minutes. They're done when golden and firm.
10 Remove and cool on a wire rack.
11 Clean down your bench, wash out the piping bag and get the next set of ingredients ready.
12 Once the profiteroles are cool, using a small knife gently make a small hole on the underside of each of them. Inside should be mainly air.
13 Using your stand mixer or an electric whisk, whip the cream. Transfer to the piping bag and pipe into the centre of each profiterole.
14 Place the chocolate in a wide bowl or plate over a pan of barely simmering water (ensuring it doesn't touch it) and gently melt.
15 Arrange the profiteroles on a serving plate and pour the chocolate sauce over them. Serve at once.

Chocolate eclairs

The *Chambers Dictionary*, much beloved by crossword setters, describes the eclair thus: 'a cake, long in shape but short in duration'. Essentially they're an elongated profiterole.

INGREDIENTS

For the pastry
- 250ml water
- 100g unsalted butter
- 150g plain flour
- 3 eggs
- Teaspoon of salt and sugar

For the filling and the coating
- 300ml of whipping cream
- 150g of milk chocolate

You do need a piping bag to make these, with a wide 1.5 or 2cm nozzle. If you've not got one you can cobble one together using something like a ziplock bag with a corner snipped off.

These amounts should give you 15–18 eclairs, depending on how long you make them.

METHOD

1 Preheat the oven to 200°C.
2 Prepare your equipment. Fit the nozzle to the piping bag and grease two large baking trays with vegetable oil.
3 Place the butter and water in a pan and heat until the butter has melted. Bring up to a rolling boil then remove from the heat on to a firm surface.
4 Add the flour to the pan and beat into the liquid with a wooden spoon.
5 Continue beating until the mixture doesn't stick to the side of the pan and forms a ball. There should be no clumps of flour remaining.
6 Leave until cool enough to handle, then give the pastry a final beating to release any remaining heat.
7 Add the beaten eggs a bit at a time, making sure you incorporate fully before adding the next bit. Your dough should be shiny and drop off the spoon reluctantly.
8 Transfer to your piping bag and pipe 15cm lengths on to both of the trays, leaving room for them to expand.
9 Bake in the oven for 10–15 minutes before reducing the temperature to 160°C and baking for a further 10 minutes. They're done when golden and firm.
10 Remove and cool on a wire rack.
11 Clean down your bench, wash out the piping bag and get the next set of ingredients ready.
12 Once the eclairs are cool, using a small knife gently slit down one side of each eclair. Inside should be mainly air.
13 Using your stand mixer or an electric whisk, whip the cream. Transfer to the piping bag and pipe into the centre of each eclair in a long line.
14 Place the chocolate in a wide bowl or plate over a pan of barely simmering water (ensuring it doesn't touch it) and gently melt.
15 Carefully dip the top of each eclair in the melted chocolate and leave to set. Keep cool until needed.

Chocolate chip cookies

A firm family favourite, particularly with a glass of milk after coming home from school. The cookie is said to have been invented in the 1930s by one Ruth Graves Wakefield, owner of the Toll House Inn in Whitman, Massachusetts, and they were originally known as Toll House cookies.

INGREDIENTS

- 125g of unsalted butter
- 150g of soft brown sugar
- 200g of plain flour
- 1 teaspoon of baking powder
- 1 teaspoon of vanilla extract
- 1 egg, beaten
- Small pinch of salt
- 200g of dark chocolate chips

Once you've mastered the basic mixture you can add all sorts of flavourings, swap the chocolate for nuts, add a spoon of peanut butter, or even M&Ms.

METHOD

1 Preheat the oven to 170°C.
2 Line two baking trays with baking parchment.
3 Put the butter and sugar in a stand mixer with the beater attachment fitted and beat until creamed together. Beat in the vanilla extract, the salt and the egg. Sieve in the flour, then the chocolate chips and lastly the baking powder and combine with a spoon.
4 Using a teaspoon, place small blobs of the mixture on the baking trays, leaving 4cm between each blob. Lightly press down with the back of the spoon to flatten a little.
5 Bake for 8–10 minutes until golden but still a little gooey in the middle.
6 Remove and cool on a wire rack.

Jammy dodgers

Now we're talking – a real tea-time classic. They're dead easy to make, being essentially two biscuits (the top one with a hole cut in it) held together with jam. What's more, making your own allows you to not only get creative with the size and shape you cut, but also the type of jam you use. In fact it doesn't have to even be jam.

INGREDIENTS

- 220g of plain flour
- 190g of butter
- 70g of caster sugar
- 1 egg yolk
- 1 teaspoon of vanilla extract
- Pinch of salt
- 3 tablespoons of jam

The brand Jammie Dodgers bought in the shops is made by Burton's Biscuit Company in Wales (they also make Wagon Wheels). The name was apparently inspired by Roger the Dodger in the *Beano* comic, and they're Doctor Who's favourite biscuit.

The dough is just the shortbread dough from page 104 enriched with an egg yolk and a little vanilla extract.

METHOD

1 Lightly grease two baking sheets.
2 Place the butter and flour in a food processor and blitz until it resembles fine breadcrumbs. Add the sugar and the egg yolk and blitz again until fully combined. Turn out on to a lightly floured work surface and knead a little to bring it together. Squash into a lozenge shape and chill for 15 minutes.

3 Preheat the oven to 160°C.
4 Working quickly, roll out into a square just over 0.5cm thick.
5 A 6cm cutter is a good standard, but you can use whatever you like.
6 Cut an equal number of discs and place on both the trays. Then, using either a 3cm round cutter or any other shape cutter you have, cut a hole out of the centre of one set of discs.
7 Place both baking sheets in the fridge to firm up a little.
8 Bake in the oven for 10–12 minutes until pale and golden, and then transfer to wire rack to cool.
9 To assemble, place a teaspoon of jam (or Nutella, or peanut butter) on the whole discs and smooth out a little, then place the holed disc on top and squash together. Carefully dust with icing sugar.

Rocky road

A great one for kids as it doesn't require any baking, just melting butter and chocolate on the hob (or even in the microwave). It's also highly customisable, meaning you can add all sorts to it such as fruit, nuts, biscuits and seeds, as well as the obligatory marshmallows. I know of one person who's even experimented with a sort of savoury version featuring nuts and cooked smoked bacon.

INGREDIENTS

- 100g of unsalted butter
- 225g of plain 70% chocolate
- 2 tablespoons of golden syrup
- 1 teaspoon of treacle (optional – I like it but kids might not)
- 100g of small marshmallow pieces
- 200g of biscuits such as digestives or ginger nuts, broken into small pieces

METHOD

1 Line a shallow baking tray with two pieces of greaseproof paper or baking parchment so that all the sides are covered. Put the biscuits in a large plastic bag and gently smash with a rolling pin into 5p-sized pieces.

2 Melt the butter, chocolate and golden syrup (and treacle if using) in a pan until combined and leave to cool slightly.

3 Add the marshmallows and biscuits to the melted chocolate and stir, then transfer to the lined baking tray.

4 Place in the fridge until set, then cut into pieces with a knife dipped in boiling water.

Fudge

Every gift shop, seaside town and tourist attraction in Britain sells fudge, so you'd imagine it'd be as English as tuppence. In fact it was first made in America in the 1880s. It's not baked in an oven, but I've included it because (a) you set it in a baking tray and (b) it's delicious.

INGREDIENTS
- 397g can of condensed milk
- 150ml of milk
- 450g of brown sugar
- 115g of butter

Once you've mastered the basic recipe you can get creative with additional flavours like vanilla, coffee, chocolate, sea salt and even peanut butter.

If you've got a sugar thermometer, and who hasn't, you'll need to heat the fudge to around 115°C. If not, have a bowl of cold water standing by, and after 10–15 minutes of boiling (a word of warning – you're dealing with molten sugar here, so be careful), drop it into the water. The fudge should roll into a soft ball.

METHOD
1 Lightly grease a square 20cm baking tin with vegetable oil.
2 Place all the ingredients in a high-sided heavy-bottomed pan and put on a low heat, stirring constantly until the sugar has dissolved.

3 Bring the mixture to the boil (you might want to don your oven gloves for this bit) then simmer for 10–15 minutes, stirring all the while so it doesn't catch on the bottom of the pan.
4 Test to see if it's ready by using a teaspoon to drop a small amount into the cold water.
5 If you're happy with it, remove from the heat and beat with a wooden spoon for 10 minutes (this is arm-aching stuff) or transfer to your stand mixer and beat with the beater attachment for 5–8 minutes. You want it to thicken up so it resembles stiff peanut butter.
6 Pour into the greased tin and place in the fridge to cool for 20 minutes or so (don't leave it there for too long, however). Cut into squares using a knife dipped in hot water. It'll keep for a few days in an airtight tub.

Biscotti

These little Italian biscuits can be knocked up lickety split, and are great to nibble on with everything from coffee to cocktails. Biscuit means 'twice baked', because you part bake the dough as a whole piece before thinly slicing and baking hard into individual biscuits.

INGREDIENTS
- 275g of plain flour
- 150g of caster sugar
- 1 teaspoon of baking powder
- 2 eggs, beaten
- A little lemon zest
- 150g of mixed nuts or other additional flavourings

You can go mustang with extra ingredients: almonds, pistachio, pecan, hazelnuts, cranberries, even chocolate chips. The main piece of advice is think what drink you're planning to serve with it, because chocolate isn't going to work as well with traditional pairings like vin santo (an Italian dessert wine) or even a sweet sherry like Pedro Ximénez; it's great with something like an espresso or hot chocolate, however.

METHOD
1. Preheat oven to 160°C, and line two baking trays with baking parchment.
2. If using nuts, toast them a little in a dry frying pan to bring out the flavour. Don't let them burn, however.
3. Combine the flour, sugar and baking powder in a stand mixer bowl with the K-beater fitted.
4. Add the toasted nuts or dried fruit, followed by the lemon zest and lastly the eggs.
5. Blend the mixture together on a low speed until you have a firm dough.
6. Roll into a sausage shape, place the dough on one of the baking trays and squash down the top a little with a chopping board.
7. Bake in the oven for 20–25 minutes.
8. Remove and leave until cool enough to handle.
9. Using a bread knife, saw – don't cut – the dough into 1cm thick slices on an angle.
10. Lay these slices on both baking trays and bake again for a further 10 minutes.
11. Cool the biscotti on a wire rack.

Muffins

Once you've mastered the basic muffin mix you can add pretty much anything to it, from chocolate to spices, fruit to cheese, often with just a minor tweak of the recipe. I've gone for the classic blueberry here.

One thing you will need is muffin tray. Look for these in the baking section of supermarkets. Also, you might want to consider paper cases for your muffins.

Finally it's very important not to overmix the batter – just swirl loosely together. The odd lump here and there is fine.

INGREDIENTS

- 300g of self-raising flour
- 1 teaspoon of baking powder
- 120g of light brown sugar
- 120g of unsalted butter, melted and cooled
- 140ml of milk
- 2 eggs, beaten
- 1 teaspoon of vanilla extract
- Large handful of fresh blueberries, about 150g

METHOD

1 Preheat the oven to 180°C.
2 Grease a muffin tray with vegetable oil or melted butter.
3 Place the flour, baking powder and sugar in a bowl. Make a well in the centre and add the melted butter, beaten eggs and vanilla and loosely combine.
4 Finally stir in the blueberries and spoon into the muffin tray.
5 Bake for around 20 minutes until the muffins look golden brown.
6 Leave for 5 minutes to cool before removing and cooling on a wire rack.

Brandy snaps

Traditionally there's no brandy in brandy snaps. The origin of the name is unclear. It first appeared in John Trotter Brockett's *A Glossary of North Country Words* in 1825, where it was suggested that it's perhaps a corruption of branding (as in with a hot iron). The good news is that if you do want a drop of hooch in your brandy snap, you can add it. You can also add a drop of Grand Marnier and the zest of an orange to the cream as I've done here. The recipe couldn't be easier, it's just 50g of everything. The knack is in shaping the snaps quickly as they cool down.

INGREDIENTS

For the brandy snaps

- 50g of butter
- 50g of demerara sugar
- 50g of golden syrup
- 50g of plain flour
- 1 teaspoon of ginger
- 1 teaspoon of cinnamon

For the brandy cream

- 300ml carton of double cream
- 1 tablespoon of Grand Marnier
- Zest of half an orange
- 2 teaspoons of icing sugar
- Handful of fresh raspberries (optional)

METHOD

1 Preheat the oven to 160°C and lay a sheet of baking parchment on two baking trays.

2 Place the butter, sugar and golden syrup in a pan and place on a very low heat for around 10 minutes. You want to ensure that all the sugar has thoroughly melted. The mixture should be smooth and shiny.

3 Take it off the heat and let it cool a little before adding the flour. Beat together to fully combine.

4 Place a dessertspoon of the mixture on the baking parchment, around 8cm across. You should have enough mixture to make around a dozen. Allow plenty of space between each one, as they'll almost double in size as they cook.

5 Place in the oven and cook until they've expanded and flattened and have a lace-like pattern on the top.

6 While they're cooking, prepare your mould. If you're making cigar-shaped brandy snaps, oil a wooden spoon handle. If you're making brandy baskets, use a small satsuma or egg cup as a mould.

7 They'll be too hot and floppy to work with straight out of the oven – wait a few minutes until they start to firm up again as the sugars set. You'll need to work quickly to shape them all around the spoon. Make sure the frilly lace-like side is facing outwards.

8 If they set too much, a quick spell in the warm oven makes them flexible again. Once you've shaped them leave them to cool before filling.

9 To make the brandy cream, whip the cream and icing sugar until it will form peaks – don't over-whip it. Then quickly fold in the zest and Grand Marnier. Transfer to a piping bag fitted with a nozzle small enough to fit in your curled brandy snaps and fill each one. Add a few fresh raspberries for colour and serve immediately.

Brownies

Do you remember when you saw your first brownie? Like many things, they just crept into our cafes and restaurants sometime in the late '80s or early '90s. Which is odd, because they've been around in the USA for a hundred years.

INGREDIENTS

- 100g of unsalted butter
- 150g of dark chocolate
- 100g of plain flour
- 200g of golden caster sugar
- 2 tablespoons of cocoa powder
- 3 eggs, beaten
- 1 teaspoon of baking powder

There are two schools of thought on brownies: the cakey kind, and the chewy, gooey kind. Me, I'm in the latter camp. I like a dark gooey centre with a light chocolate crust. This crust is made by beating the batter after you've added the eggs.

METHOD

1 Preheat the oven to 160°C.
2 Grease and line a rectangular or square baking tin with baking paper.
3 Place a large bowl over a pan of barely simmering water (ensuring it doesn't touch it) and add the chocolate and melt.
4 In a stand mixer, beat the butter and sugar together until the mixture is soft and creamy.
5 Add the eggs gradually and combine each one, then the flour and the cocoa powder and baking powder. Finally add the melted chocolate and combine thoroughly.
6 Pour into the lined tin and bake in the oven for 25–30 minutes, until firm to the touch. Check with a cake skewer – if it comes out clean they're done.
7 Leave to cool in the tin then remove and cut into squares. You can also give them a final dusting of cocoa powder.

Hazelnut spread brownies

Possibly the easiest brownie recipe on the planet, given that it only has three ingredients, they are...

- 300g of Nutella or other chocolate spread
- 2 eggs
- 60g of plain flour

1 Mix everything together well in a bowl.
2 Place in a greased and lined baking tray and bake at 160°C for 25 minutes.
3 Leave to cool a little before cutting into portions

Eccles cakes

One Mr James Birch is often said to have popularised Eccles cakes in the town of Eccles, Lancashire, in the late 1790s, and they've been a firm favourite ever since. They're known locally as 'dead fly pies', because of the currants in them. In my travels I've eaten a lot of Eccles cakes, include ones from the town itself, and I have to say that the best I've ever had wasn't there, but at the Pump Street Bakery in Orford, Suffolk (they do mail order – you really should try some).

INGREDIENTS

For the filling

- Three tablespoons of Armagnac
- 100g of raisins
- 100g of currants (Voztizza are regarded as the best in the world – find them in health food shops)
- 50g of unsalted butter
- 100g of soft dark brown sugar
- 1 teaspoon of ground cinnamon
- 1 teaspoon of ground nutmeg

To glaze

- 3 beaten egg whites
- Golden caster sugar

In my opinion the currants should be contained in the centre of the pastry, not mixed throughout. The pastry should be puff, three slits should be cut in the top to let out the steam as it bakes, and there should be lots of sugar – dark, chewy, sticky sugar that melts in the oven.

Just up the road from Eccles is the town of Chorley, who have a similar cake, except theirs is made with shortcrust rather than puff pastry. It also lacks the sugary dusting, and is instead sometimes served smeared with butter.

Puff pastry is a bit of a faff to make, but if you want to stay 'match fit' and have a go, turn to page 49. Otherwise just buy in a good all-butter one. You'll need about 300g.

METHOD

1 First make the filling. Place the raisins and currants in a bowl and pour the Armagnac over them. Leave to soak overnight. The next day melt the butter and sugar in a saucepan and add the drained fruits and spices. Leave to cool.

2 Have your work area cool and pastry ready. Gently roll out the pastry and cut 8–10 10cm discs. If you've not got a cutter big enough, use a bowl or a saucer and cut round with a knife.

3 Place a large spoonful of the filling in the centre of the pastry disc, brush the edge all around with water and fold on the four edges, as it were. Press firmly together to seal, then turn over and make three slashes with a sharp knife or scalpel.

4 Repeat for the remaining discs then place them all back in the fridge to chill for another 40 minutes.

5 Preheat your oven to 220°C.

6 Take the cakes out of the fridge and dip the slashed top side in the beaten egg white, then in the caster sugar. Place on a baking tray lined with baking parchment and place in the hot oven for 15–20 minutes until the pastry has puffed up and the sugar melted. Don't worry if a little bit of the filling bubbles up or out of the slashes.

7 Serve with a big wedge of Lancashire cheese.

CHAPTER 6
PIES AND TARTS

Nearly all of these recipes require a good blind-baked pastry case. If you can do that without it shrinking, bubbling up or crumbling then you're well on your way to becoming a proficient baker. From summer fruit tarts to festive mince pies, there's something for all year round.

Apple pie

A man can devote a lifetime to endlessly striving for the perfect apple pie. After all, there are so many variables: the type of pastry, the type of apple, the ideal shape and structure. And finally, ice cream or custard?

INGREDIENTS

For the filling
- 4 big Bramley apples (about 1kg)
- 2 dessert apples
- 30g of caster sugar
- Pinch of cinnamon (two if you like it)
- Pinch of nutmeg
- Tablespoon of apple juice (or cider, thinking about it!)
- Teaspoon of cornflour (optional depending on the ripeness of your apples – see method)

For the pastry
- 400g of plain flour
- 100g of butter
- 100g of lard
- 30g of caster sugar
- Pinch of salt
- A few tablespoons of cold water

Here's how I like to make mine. Pastry has to be homely shortcrust – puff just doesn't work here. Also I like to use lard in my sweet shortcrust – if the idea is strange to you, substitute an equal amount of butter. The apples, I feel, need to be a combination of mainly cookers (Bramleys) and a few dessert. The former mush down to almost a sauce, while the latter stay firm to provide a filling. And it most definitely has to be custard to serve with it, or cream at a push. This is a double crust pie.

Apple pie is best served warm, rather than piping hot from the oven. So allow plenty of time to make it. This should make enough for a round 9in/23cm pie tin. As with most recipes, adjust your pastry and filling to fit your dish.

METHOD

1 Make the shortcrust pastry by putting the flour and sugar in a bowl and rubbing in the fat, then add a little water and combine to form a dough. Bring together and squash into a lozenge shape, wrap in cling film and chill.

2 Peel and core the Bramleys and cut into chunks. Peel and core the dessert apples and slice as thinly as you can. Place the Bramleys in a saucepan with a drizzle of apple juice, cider or even water to stop them sticking and put on a low heat. Add the sugar. Watch them, as Bramleys will turn to mush on a sixpence.

3 Now, how watery is your apple mix? If your apples are particularly ripe or if you prefer a firmer filling you might want to add a little cornflour to thicken and set your filling. When you're happy with it and the Bramleys have begun to mush down, add the slices of dessert apple and gently push down into the Bramley mush. Cook for another few minutes. Remember, it'll set a little when it cools, so put the lid on and leave to cool. You're after a balance of tartness from the Bramleys and sweetness from the dessert apples.

4 Get the oven up to 180°C. Beat one egg in a cup and have it standing by. Remove a third of the pastry and place back in the fridge. Roll out the remaining two-thirds to line your pie dish. Don't cut the overhanging excess, just neaten it up so you can get it in the oven. With a pastry brush, paint the pastry with the beaten egg. This will help stop any apple juices from leaking into your pastry. Place the tin in the hot oven for a few moments (3–4 minutes) to set the egg, then remove.

5 Place the filling into the pie, trim the excess pastry and roll out the remaining third of the pastry. Use the rest of the beaten egg to seal the lid on to the pie. Brush the lid with the rest of the egg and dust over some more caster sugar. Cut a small hole in the top to let any steam out.

6 Place in the oven and cook for 45–50 minutes until golden brown. Remove and let cool for a good 20 minutes before you even think about cutting it.

7 Serve with custard (page 57), obviously.

Optional extras

There's an old saying that 'an apple without cheese is like a kiss without a squeeze'. If you'd like to introduce cheese to your apple pie you can either add 50g of grated cheddar to the pastry, or a crumbly cheese like Wensleydale to the apple mix. Needless to say I'd avoid serving with custard if you go down this route.

Cherry pie

'Kent, sir – everybody knows Kent – apples, cherries, hops and women,' said Charles Dickens of that county. Sadly Kent doesn't produce as much of the first three as it used to any more, though travelling through the county in midsummer you can often see people in a lay-by selling cherries. Sussex and Hertfordshire are two other big cherry-producing counties in the South-East.

INGREDIENTS

For the pastry
- 400g of plain flour
- 100g of butter
- 100g of lard
- Pinch of salt
- 30g of caster sugar (and a sprinkle more for on top)
- A few tablespoons of cold water
- Beaten egg to glaze

For the filling
- 500g of stoned cherries
- Teaspoon of booze (kirsch or brandy)
- 1 tablespoon of cornflour
- 20g of caster sugar

Cherries have a short season, just two months, July and August. Consequently this is one of those pies that you should only make if you happen on a glut of them. You need at least a good-sized boxful, 500g at least. Look out for sour cherries such as Morello rather than dessert ones.

If you're going to have a go, I'd also recommend a cherry stoner, which can be had for about a fiver online, as de-stoning a kilogram of cherries by hand with a knife will send you insane. Alternatively you could use tinned cherries. Just don't try it with the glacé variety.

I think a shallow pie dish similar to a plate works best for this, but use whatever dish you're comfortable with.

METHOD

1 Make the sweet shortcrust pastry by putting the flour and sugar in a bowl and rubbing in the fat, then add a little water and combine to form a dough. Bring together and squash into a lozenge shape, wrap in cling film and chill. Alternatively make it in a food processor, or use ready-made. Get your oven up to 180°C.

2 Mix the stoned cherries, cornflour and sugar together in a saucepan and heat gently. You don't want them to turn to mush, just soften them up a bit. The cornflour should help thicken the sauce. Once they're softened, set aside to cool.

3 Cut off a third of the pastry and reserve for the lid. Roll out the remainder and line your pie dish. Prick the bottom with a fork, line with baking parchment, tip on your baking beads and blind bake for 7–8 minutes.

4 Remove and brush with beaten egg, return to the oven for a minute to set the egg. Trim off any excess or overhang.

5 Place your cool cherry filling into the pie dish and brush the lip with beaten egg. Roll out the lid and place on top, crimping it carefully to the base. Brush with the rest of the beaten egg and sprinkle over some sugar.

Treacle tart

The word treacle comes from the Greek *theriake*, which means an antidote to venom. These were often administered with something sweet like honey to aid digestion. Of course, the word now means the syrup produced as a by-product of sugar manufacturing.

INGREDIENTS

For the pastry case

- 400g of plain flour
- 100g of butter
- 100g of lard
- Pinch of salt
- A few tablespoons of cold water

For the filling

- 300g of soft breadcrumbs
- Juice of half a lemon
- 400g of golden syrup
- A tablespoon of black treacle

Sugar is made from boiled and refined sugar cane, or today sugar beet. What's left used to be thrown away, until Abram Lyle found a way to refine this, giving us golden syrup. It was a sort of honey substitute for urban industrial Victorian Britain. It was very popular with poorer families as it was incredibly sweet, and the principal ingredient was stale bread.

In 1950 black treacle was launched, which has a stronger, slightly bitter flavour that I love. Most recipes for treacle tart suggest using just golden syrup.

However, I like to cut it with black treacle as it makes things a little more interesting; it also helps dial down the teeth-ripping sweetness of the syrup, as does the lemon juice. The case is a standard shortcrust (page 44), only I've removed the caster sugar as there's enough sweet stuff in this recipe as it is.

Incidentally, Tate & Lyle's iconic green and gold can has barely changed since it was first introduced in 1884. Indeed, when metrification was brought in they just changed from selling 1lb tins to 454g ones.

METHOD

1 Make the pastry case first (page 44) by rubbing in the butter, lard and flour until they resemble breadcrumbs or blitzing in a food processor. Add the salt, then the water and combine to make your dough.

2 Flour your bench and transfer the dough. Begin rolling out, turning the dough 90° after every roll.

3 Roll gently over your pin and transfer to your tart dish. Using a scrap of pastry, push gently into the corners. Chill for 30 minutes. Preheat the oven to 190°C.

4 Line the pastry with four pieces of cling film (page 18) or scrunched-up baking parchment and weigh down with baking beads.

5 Blind bake for 10–15 minutes and then remove the cling film or baking paper and return to the oven for a few minutes.

6 To make the filling, place a saucepan on your scales and weigh out the syrup and treacle. Warm them on the hob ever so slightly (this makes it easier to pour into the pastry case). Then add the breadcrumbs and lemon juice and combine.

7 Pour the filling into the blind-baked pastry case and return to the oven for another 20 minutes until cooked.

8 Best served as is, or with custard or cream. I wouldn't recommend ice cream, as it can cause the filling to harden again, meaning it becomes crunchy.

Portuguese custard tarts

These little tarts are known as *pastéis de nata* in their native Portugal, and they've become a bit of a hit here in the UK. One bakery I know in South London makes over 15,000 a week.

INGREDIENTS
- 1 egg and 2 egg yolks
- 125g of caster sugar
- 30g of cornflour
- 220ml of double cream
- 170ml of full fat milk
- 1 vanilla pod with the seeds scraped out
- 1 packet (375g) of pre-made puff pastry
- Butter for greasing

Commercial ovens can reach 300°C and cook the little tarts in under 12 minutes. That's a little tricky to do in a domestic oven, but you'll need to get yours as hot as it can go. The trick is to cut the pastry in half, place one piece on top of the other, roll the pastry up into a cylinder and cut into 3cm coils. These are then pressed into a muffin tray. It's this process that gives *pastéis de nata* their distinctive leafy crinkly edges.

METHOD

1 Put the egg yolks, sugar and cornflour in a pan, add the milk and cream and mix thoroughly together. Place the pan on a low heat and stir gently until it begins to thicken. When it does, turn out the heat and cover with cling film to prevent a skin forming. Leave to cool.

2 Preheat oven to 220°C.

3 Lightly grease a 12-hole muffin tray with butter.

4 Take your puff pastry from the packet and cut in half widthways. Place one piece on top of the other and roll up into a tube. Using your sharpest knife, cut 3cm discs from the pastry. Roll each disc a little with a rolling pin to flatten to around 8–10cm and place into the muffin tin. Place the tin back in the fridge for 15–20 minutes to chill down the pastry.

5 When you're ready to make them, pour the custard in a small jug or something with a spout (this will help you accurately pour it into the waiting pastry rather than trying to do it from the pan).

6 Fill each pastry case two-thirds full and then take to the oven. Once on the shelf, top up with the remaining custard (you don't have to do this if you think you can get the fully-filled tarts from the bench to the oven shelf without any spilling over).

7 Bake for 15–20 minutes until the custard has set and caramelised and the pastry puffed up and out. Once cool, dust with a small amount of icing sugar and serve.

Mince pies

Mince pies are to be found everywhere at Christmas time, from budget versions to fancy filled ones, but you can't beat rubbing up your own batch for when the hordes descend. These are the pies to get your novelty cutters out, so you can play around with the tops. Also, I'd recommend adding a drop of brandy to the mincemeat. Kids hate mince pies anyway, so you don't have to worry about them. You could also add more fruit, and chocolate chips too (not traditional, but nice). You'll need a 12-pie tray.

INGREDIENTS
- 500g of shortcrust pastry (see page 44)
- 350g of mincemeat
- Slug of brandy
- Caster sugar for dusting
- Milk

METHOD
1 Roll out the pastry, and using a 2in cutter cut 12 discs and place in the tray. Gather the remaining pastry, roll out again, and cut 12 lids with a slightly smaller cutter.
2 Place a dessertspoon of mincemeat in each bottom case. Brush a little milk around the rim of each pie and place a lid on.
3 Dust with the caster sugar and bake in a hot oven (180°C) for 15–20 minutes. Apply a little more caster sugar.
4 Best served warm with drinks, friends and relatives.

Chocolate tart

Despite being surprisingly easy to make, this chocolate tart is still impressive when brought to the table. The pastry case can be made in advance. After that it's just a simple ganache (page 59) helped along with a few extra flavours.

INGREDIENTS
- 350g of shortcrust pastry (either ready-made or made from scratch – page 44)
- 250ml of double cream
- ½ teaspoon of vanilla extract
- 50g of caster sugar
- 50g of unsalted butter at room temperature
- 50ml of full fat milk
- 400g of dark chocolate, 70% cocoa solids or more

METHOD
1. Preheat the oven to 160°C.
2. Lightly grease a shallow 23cm tart tin.
3. Roll out the pastry and line the tin.
4. Place 3 or 4 sheets of cling film or a sheet of scrunched-up baking parchment on the pastry and fill with baking beads.
5. Bake in the oven for 15 minutes until pale and golden, then remove the beads and cling film or paper and bake for approximately 10 more minutes. Leave to cool. (Up to this point everything can be done in advance.)
6. Place the cream, butter, sugar, milk and vanilla extract in a large pan and bring to the boil. Remove from the heat and add the chocolate. Stir gently until melted and fully combined.
7. Pour into the cooled pastry case and chill in the fridge for at least 2 hours.
8. To serve, remove from the tin and slice with a knife dipped in hot water. Dust with a little caster sugar when on the plate.

Tarte Tatin

There's always a story attached to how dishes came to be invented, and you can rest assured that mishap and error aren't far behind. So it is with tarte Tatin, apparently brought into the world by the Tatin sisters in their hotel in France when an apple pie somehow went wrong and they flipped it out of the dish and tried to pass it off. Well, you would wouldn't you? Lo and behold, everyone loved it rather than saying 'What the hell's this mess?', and the rest is history. You can Tatin anything really: tomatoes or sausages, for instance; you can use pears or plums instead of apples, while bananas and rum would be a nice combination too. You'll need a small oven-proof frying pan (20cm) for this.

INGREDIENTS

- 160g of ready-made puff pastry
- 100g of butter
- 10ml of water
- 100g of caster sugar
- 8 Cox's apples, peeled, cored and halved

METHOD

1 Prepare the apples. (You can do this a day ahead and store them in the fridge. They'll turn brown, but they're going to get caramelised anyway.)

2 Put the butter, water and sugar in the pan on a high heat until the sugar starts to melt and go golden brown. You're after a caramel. Turn the heat down and add the apple halves. You may need to break up a few to fill in the gaps.

3 Preheat the oven to 200°C.

4 Roll out the pastry to about 0.5cm thick and, using a small plate just a bit bigger than your pan, cut a round disc. Place this on top of the apples and tuck the edges down inside the pan. Cook for 25–30 minutes until the pastry has risen up then leave to cool for five minutes. Carefully invert on to a plate and serve, still warm, with some cream.

Tarte au citron

A French classic, nice and tart (in the English sense of the word). With that sharp lemon and rich buttery pastry it's a pudding with Parisian style and finesse.

INGREDIENTS

For the pastry
- 300g of plain flour
- 150g of butter cut into cubes and at room temperature
- 30g of caster sugar
- 2 eggs, beaten
- A few teaspoons of cold water

For the filling
- 2 eggs
- 100g of caster sugar
- 150ml of double cream
- Juice and zest of two lemons
- 50g of unsalted butter, melted

METHOD

1 Put the flour in a bowl and add the butter. Using your fingertips, gently rub together until combined and resembling breadcrumbs. Add the sugar and stir, then most of the eggs (save about a quarter to seal the pastry later after blind baking) and as much water as you need to bring it together into a dough.

2 Knead lightly on a floured surface until smooth, then squash into a lozenge, wrap in cling film and place in the fridge for 40 minutes.

3 After resting, on a floured surface roll out the pastry into a circle bigger than a 23cm fluted tart tin. Place the pastry in the tin and drape the excess over the edges. Put back in the fridge to chill again.

4 Preheat the oven to 170°C.

5 Line the pastry with baking parchment (or cling film – see page 18) and fill with baking beads. Trim the excess pastry off.

6 Bake in the oven for 15 minutes then remove. Brush with the remaining egg to form a barrier between the pastry and where the filling will go. Turn the oven off, but return the pastry to it briefly to just cook the egg.

7 You're going to be putting quite a wet filling on this, so to avoid the dreaded soggy bottom do make sure your pastry is properly blind baked.

To make the filling

8 Put the sugar, eggs, cream, lemon zest and juice in a bowl and whisk until it resembles cream. Add the melted butter and whisk into the lemon mixture.

9 Pour this into the blind-baked pastry case and bake for 15 minutes in the oven. Then reduce the oven to 160°C and continue to cook for another 15–20 minutes until the filling has set to a wobble.

10 Take out and leave to cool completely. Dust with a smidgen of icing sugar before slicing and serving.

Gypsy tart

No one is sure how or when gypsy tart was invented. Don't let anyone fool you into thinking it's some old farmhouse recipe – there's nothing 'farmy' about using a can of condensed milk. As usual in the food history there are tales, but nothing certain. The 'where', however, seems to be Kent. But this may only be because various celebs, chefs and food writers from that county now in the public eye had it at school. It is, by today's standards, teeth-strippingly sweet. Which means kids love it.

INGREDIENTS
- 1 packet of ready-made shortcrust pastry
- 410g can of evaporated milk, chilled in the fridge overnight (this is really important)
- 350g of dark muscovado sugar

You can lovingly make a shortcrust pastry case by hand, but for this recipe I wouldn't bother – just use ready-made pastry.

METHOD

1 Preheat the oven to 170°C.
2 Dust the worktop and roll out the pastry. Place in a 23cm tart tin and trim off the excess.
3 Cover with cling film or baking parchment and fill with baking beads.
4 Bake in the oven until pale and golden.
5 Remove the cling film or parchment and return to the oven for 5 minutes. You want this pretty much fully baked rather than blind baked, as the filling doesn't need much cooking, just setting.
6 Place the chilled evaporated milk and sugar in a bowl. If using a stand mixer fit the balloon whisk attachment, or use a handheld whisk.
7 The key is in the whisking. You need to whisk it for around 15 minutes. You want to dissolve the sugar and get the milk nice and bubbly. Test it – if it's still gritty, keep whisking.
8 Fill the pastry case two-thirds full, then place in the oven on a shelf, then transfer the rest of the milk mixture to a small jug and top up in the oven.
9 Bake for 3–5 minutes, then check the filling by giving it a little nudge. When it's set to a wobble, it's done.
10 Serve with *crème fraîche*.

Key lime pie

Key limes are distinctly different to the more familiar and larger Persian limes, and are as rare as hen's teeth in the UK. Their name comes from the fact that they were grown around the Florida Keys. Unless you're planning a trip to Disneyland soon, probably best to use ordinary Persian limes.

INGREDIENTS

For the pastry
- 400g of plain flour
- 100g of butter
- 100g of lard
- 30g of caster sugar
- Pinch of salt
- A few tablespoons of cold water

For the filling
- 4 egg yolks
- 395g of tinned condensed milk
- 120ml of lime juice
- Zest of a lime
- Icing sugar for dusting

METHOD

1 Make the pastry case first (page 44) by rubbing in the butter, lard and flour until they resemble breadcrumbs, or make in a stand mixer using the K-beater attachment. Add the salt, then the water and combine to make your dough.

2 Flour your bench and transfer the dough to it. Begin rolling out, turning the dough 90° after every roll.

3 Roll gently over your pin and transfer to your tart dish. Using a scrap of pastry, push gently into the corners. Trim off the excess and chill for 30 minutes.

4 Preheat the oven to 190°C.

5 Line the pastry with four pieces of cling film (page 18) or scrunched-up baking parchment and weigh down with baking beads.

6 Blind bake for 10–15 minutes and then remove the cling film or baking paper and return to the oven for a few minutes. Leave to cool.

To make the filling

7 Heat the oven to 160°C.

8 Beat together the egg yolks, condensed milk, lime juice and zest in your mixer until fully combined.

9 Pour into the cooled pie case and smooth down the surface with a palette knife.

10 Bake in the oven for 20–25 minutes or until the filling is set.

11 Remove and leave to cool, then store in the fridge.

12 When ready to serve, dust with a little icing sugar and serve with whipped cream.

Fruit tart

During the summer months, and even into autumn, this recipe lets you make the most of whatever berries and fruits are available. Popular toppings include strawberries, raspberries, blackberries and blueberries, or even a combination of all of the above. Just don't use anything too heavy or it will sink into the *crème* part.

INGREDIENTS

For the pastry case
- 400g of plain flour
- 100g of butter
- 100g of lard
- Pinch of salt
- A few tablespoons of cold water

For the crème pâtissière
- 4 egg yolks
- 80g of golden caster sugar
- 25g of cornflour
- 1 vanilla pod
- 350ml of milk

Topping
- 20 strawberries, or around 500g of mixed berries and fruits
- Warmed strawberry jam to glaze

METHOD

1 Make the pastry case first (page 44) by rubbing in the butter, lard and flour until they resemble breadcrumbs or blitzing in a food processor. Add the salt, then the water and combine to make your dough.

2 Flour your bench and transfer the dough. Begin rolling out, turning the dough 90° after every roll. Chill for an hour.

3 Roll gently over your pin and transfer to your loose-bottomed tart dish. Using a scrap of pastry, push gently into the corners. Chill for 15 minutes. Preheat the oven to 190°C.

4 Line the pastry with four pieces of cling film (page 18) or scrunched-up baking parchment and weigh down with plenty of baking beads or dried beans.

5 Blind bake for 10–15 minutes and then remove the cling film or baking paper and return to the oven for another 5 minutes. You're not going to cook the pastry again so you want it fully cooked and golden brown. When it's done, leave to cool in the tin, then gently remove and slide on to a flat serving plate or cake stand.

To make the crème pâtissière

6 In a stand mixer, or using a bowl hand whisk, beat together the egg yolks and sugar. Add the flour and cornflour and mix until fully combined.

7 Split and scrape the seeds from the vanilla pod, then add to the milk in a saucepan (wash the pod and place in a jar with some sugar to make vanilla sugar).

8 Bring to gentle simmer, then pour half the milk into the bowl containing the egg mixture, whisking constantly. When fully combined, pour this back into the saucepan containing the rest of the milk and bring to a gentle boil for 1 minute until the *crème pâtissière* is smooth.

9 Remove from the heat and pour into a bowl to cool. Once cold, cover the bowl with cling film to stop a skin forming.

To assemble the tart

10 Remove any stalks from your fruit, or if using strawberries remove the hulls and cut into quarters.

11 Place a layer of the *crème pâtissière* in the tart case about 1cm deep, and then top with the fruit. You can glaze with a little strawberry jam, warmed in the microwave if you like. Finally dust over a little icing sugar and serve chilled.

Pecan pie

A modern American classic, and often eaten at Thanksgiving and Christmas. Many US recipes call for corn syrup, which might be tricky to track down in the UK, so use maple or golden syrup instead.

INGREDIENTS

- 100g of muscovado sugar
- 2 tablespoons of maple or golden syrup
- 100g of butter
- 3 eggs, beaten
- 300g of pecan nuts, chopped
- Handful of whole pecans for decoration
- 400g of sweet shortcrust pastry (see pages 44–45)

METHOD

1 Make the sweet shortcrust pastry by putting the flour and sugar in a bowl and rubbing in the fat, then add a little water and combine to form a dough. Bring together and squash into a lozenge shape, wrap in cling film and chill. Alternatively make it in a food processor or use ready-made. Get your oven up to 180°C.

2 Roll it out to the thickness of a pound coin, prick with a fork, and line your tin with it. Blind bake for 15 minutes until the pastry is a pale golden colour. Remove the paper. Let it cool (but leave in the tin).

3 In a bowl, mix the eggs, syrup and sugar. Melt the butter in a pan and slowly add to the eggy sugar mixture, whisking all the time. Add the chopped pecans and pour into the pastry case.

4 Bake for 40–50 minutes at 160°C until the pastry is golden and the filling set. Leave to cool a little before removing from the tin. Can be served warm or cold.

Baked cheesecake

Of course, the most well-known cheesecake in the world is the New York version, but did you know that here in Britain we have a long history of similar things? A Yorkshire curd tart, for example, is a variation of cheesecake, designed to use up leftover curds from cheese-making, and has been around since the 17th century.

Today there are two types of cheesecakes, baked ones and chilled ones. Baked ones are more custardy and velvety, while chilled ones are lighter as they rely on beaten egg white for body.

INGREDIENTS

- 150g of digestive biscuits bashed or blitzed into crumbs
- 90g of melted butter, plus a little extra for greasing
- Zest of a lemon
- 900g of full-fat cream cheese
- 250g of caster sugar
- 1 tablespoon of plain flour
- 1 teaspoon of vanilla extract
- 2 eggs and 1 extra yolk

METHOD

1 Preheat oven to 180°C.
2 Lightly grease a non-stick 23cm springform baking tin.
3 Melt the butter in the microwave or a pan and add the biscuit crumbs and the lemon zest and fully combine so that the butter coats all the crumbs.
4 Spoon into the tin and press down firmly and evenly with the back of a spoon. Place in the fridge to set.
5 In a stand mixer, beat the cream cheese, vanilla extract, flour and caster sugar. Add one egg and combine before adding the other one and finally the yolk.
6 Spoon the filling into the cake tin and spread evenly with a palette knife or a plastic spoon.
7 Bake in the oven for 45–55 minutes until set – do not open the door. Turn off the oven and leave the cheesecake in there to cool for a further hour. Then remove and chill completely. Serve with fresh blueberries.

Lemon meringue

Takes a bit of time, this one, but you can quite easily do it all in stages. You want the lemon layer to be quite tart, as it's going to have a heap of sugary meringue on top of it. This is sufficient for a 20cm tart tin. It's best to use one with a removable bottom.

INGREDIENTS

For the pastry case
- 400g of plain flour
- 100g of butter
- 100g of lard
- Pinch of salt
- A few tablespoons of cold water

For the filling
- Zest and juice of three large lemons (around 120–150ml of juice)
- 100g of caster sugar
- 2 tablespoons of cornflour
- 1 egg and 3 egg yolks beaten together (keep whites for the meringue)
- 80g of butter at room temperature cut into cubes
- 100ml of water

For the meringue
- 3 egg whites
- 200g of caster sugar
- 2 level teaspoons of cornflour

METHOD

1 Make the shortcrust pastry case first (page 44) by rubbing in the butter, lard and flour until they resemble breadcrumbs or blitzing in a food processor. Add the salt, then the water and combine to make your dough.

2 Flour your bench and transfer the dough to it. Begin rolling out, turning the dough 90° after every roll.

3 Roll gently over your pin and transfer to your tart dish. Using a scrap of pastry, push gently into the corners. Chill for 30 minutes.

4 Preheat the oven to 160°C.

5 Line the pastry with four pieces of cling film (page 18) or scrunched-up baking parchment and weigh down with baking beads.

6 Blind bake for 10–15 minutes and then remove the cling film or baking paper and return to the oven for a few minutes. This can be done in advance and left to cool completely.

Making the filling

7 Over a medium heat put the lemon juice and zest in a pan with the water and add the cornflour, stirring until fully combined. Add the sugar and the beaten egg yolks and stir until thickened, then add the butter. You're after something like thick custard.

8 When it starts to bubble take it off the heat and pour into the pastry case. Leave both to cool completely before adding the meringue.

Making the meringue

9 Get the oven back up to 170°C. Follow the preparation tips on pages 52–53. Whisk the egg whites with a balloon whisk attachment until white and foamy. Begin adding the sugar a spoon at a time and keep whisking until they're beginning to form soft peaks and the meringue looks shiny. Lastly whisk in the cornflour.

10 Spoon or pipe on to the cooled lemon topping and bake in the oven for 10–15 minutes until meringue is cooked and beginning to turn

Cheat's lemon meringue

If making the lemon curd seems a touch daunting at first, you can cheat by using the best part of a jar of good quality lemon curd – I won't judge you.

golden. Watch it like a hawk, as it can turn brown on a sixpence. You can always finish it off with a blowtorch.

11 Leave to cool, then pop the outer ring off the flan dish and serve.

Fig tart

I'm lucky enough to have a fig tree in my garden, though it only produces really good figs in the hottest of summers. However, for this recipe you don't want green figs but the dark ruby ones. Only buy them in the summer months – in the autumn, make this recipe with plums or greengages instead. Tinned fruits like pears or apricots can be used all year round.

INGREDIENTS

For the pastry
- 300g of plain flour
- 80g of butter
- 80g of lard (or 200g of butter if you prefer)
- 60g of caster sugar
- Pinch of salt
- ½ teaspoon of vanilla extract

For the frangipane filling
- 150g of unsalted butter, softened
- 150g of caster sugar
- 3 eggs, beaten
- 200g of ground almonds
- 40g of plain flour
- 5 figs (depending on size) trimmed of their stalks and cut in half or quarters
- Honey to glaze

METHOD

1 First make the pastry. Place the flour into a bowl and add the cut-up butter and lard.
2 Rub together quickly until it resembles breadcrumbs. The odd lump of butter is OK.
3 Add a tablespoon or two of very cold water and gently combine. If it's looking a little dry, add another.
4 Bring together into a ball, squash it a little, and put in a sandwich bag or cling film in the fridge for at least an hour.
5 Preheat the oven to 160°C.
6 Roll out and line your tart tin, trim off the excess pastry, prick the base with a fork, then place cling film or baking parchment over it. Fill with baking beads and blind bake for 10–12 minutes. Remove the cling film or parchment and continue to bake for another 3–4 minutes.

To make the filling

7 Beat together the butter and the sugar, add the eggs one at a time, then add the flour and finally the almonds. Mix well, then place in the pastry case (it should half-fill it – remember it'll expand as it cooks thanks to the eggs). Arrange the pieces of fig in a pattern on top of the frangipane.
8 Turn the oven up to 170°C.
9 Bake the tart for 50 minutes.
10 When the tart is cooked, leave to cool down and then melt the honey in a cup in the microwave (or in a pan) and, using a pastry brush, glaze the top of the tart. You could also scatter with some flaked almonds if you have any.

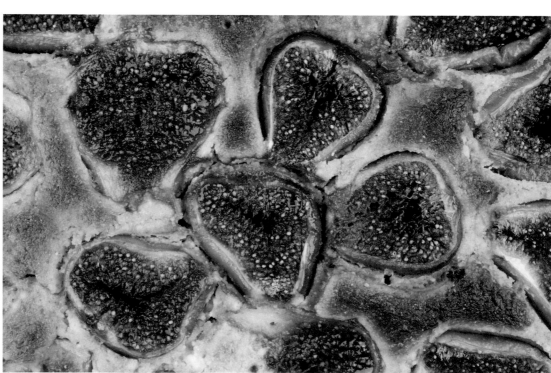

Pumpkin pie

An autumnal American classic eaten during Thanksgiving, Hallowe'en and Christmas. And yet despite being native to the Americans, the first recipes appeared this side of the Atlantic in the 17th century.

INGREDIENTS

For the pastry
- 400g of plain flour
- 100g of butter
- 100g of lard (or 200g of butter if you prefer)
- 30g of caster sugar
- Pinch of salt
- A few tablespoons of cold water

or
- 500g block of ready-made shortcrust pastry

For the filling
- 1 large butternut squash
- 1 teaspoon of cinnamon
- 1 teaspoon of nutmeg
- 1 tablespoon of honey (or maple syrup)
- 3 eggs, beaten
- 200ml of double cream

Many US recipes use tinned pumpkin, which you can now find here in the UK in larger supermarkets. However, you can also use butternut squash, which is far less watery than the familiar orange pumpkins we carve faces into.

METHOD

1 First make the pastry case (page 44) by rubbing in the butter, lard and flour until they resemble breadcrumbs, or make in a stand mixer using the K-beater attachment. Add the salt, then the water and combine to make your dough.

2 Flour your bench and transfer the dough to it. Begin rolling out, turning the dough 90° after every roll.

3 Roll gently over your pin and transfer to a 23cm tart dish. Using a scrap of pastry, push gently into the corners. Trim off the excess and chill for 30 minutes.

4 Preheat the oven to 190°C.

5 Peel the butternut squash and dice into cubes. Place on a baking tray and sprinkle over the spices. Roast in the oven for 20 minutes until soft and tender. Remove and allow to cool.

6 Back to the pastry. Line the pastry with four pieces of cling film (page 18) or scrunched-up baking parchment and weigh down with baking beads.

7 Blind bake for 10–15 minutes and then remove the cling film or baking paper and return to the oven for a few minutes. Leave to cool.

8 Place the cooled butternut squash and any sticky bits from the roasting tray into a food processor and blitz until smooth.

9 Place in a clean bowl and add the honey, the beaten eggs and the cream and mix thoroughly. You want a stiffish mixture that's still pourable.

10 Pour into the pastry case, place in the oven, and bake for 10–15 minutes until cooked. If the crust looks like it's going too brown, but the filling isn't yet fully cooked, place a strip of tin foil over the crust to protect it.

11 Allow the pie to cool on a wire rack. Serve with ice cream and perhaps a dribble of maple syrup.

CHAPTER 7

BAKED AND STEAMED PUDDINGS

Now we're talking. This is the real rib-sticking stuff chapter. Steamed puddings were the original puds, as they could be boiled in a pot over a fire. This, remember, was a time when few people had proper sealed ovens for baking. Consequently they tend to be big and filling, and are best served with lashings of custard. There's a few other curiosities in this chapter such as hollygog and clootie dumplings, which come with a long history that I think should grace our tables a bit more often.

Apple crumble

Absolute family favourite and a doddle to make, apple crumble and custard is one of those dishes that we imagine has been around for centuries. Actually it's not that old. During World War Two many of the ingredients to make pastry – butter, sugar and flour – were all rationed. Without them, making an apple pie (page 133) was tricky. So what little ingredients they had were instead used to make a topping. Once the butter was gone other fats were used, and oats could be added to bulk out the flour.

INGREDIENTS

For the topping
- 130g of plain flour
- 50g of oats
- 100g of muscovado or dark brown sugar
- 80g of unsalted butter chopped into small pieces

For the filling
- 4–6 cooking apples
- Pinch of cinnamon or nutmeg
- Teaspoon of water

The key to a good crumble is to ensure you get a good crunchy topping on top, but slightly gooey and apple stewy underneath. Too much flour and not enough fat and that won't happen. Sugar in the topping also plays a crucial role in providing crunch and sweetness.

Crumble should be about the yin and yang interplay between the soft but tart filling and the sweet but crunchy topping, therefore I tend to avoid adding sugar to the filling given that there's already plenty in the topping and the custard. However, if you're making this for kids or you've a particularly sweet tooth, add 30g or so to the stewed apples. This recipe fills an oblong dish about 25cm x 15cm and 4cm deep.

METHOD

1 Peel and core your apples and chop into chunks. Place in a saucepan, add a pinch of cinnamon, a dribble of water or apple juice, and put on a low heat for 15 minutes. When the apples start to break down, remove and leave to cool.

2 Make your topping by combining flour, oats, spices and sugar in a bowl and rubbing in the butter. It should be a sandy colour. Spoon the mixture over the cooled apple mix and bake in the oven for 30 minutes at 170°C until the top looks golden and brown.

3 Serve with custard, ice cream, cream, or all three.

Alternative method

Too much rubbing in of the butter will start to melt it, so this recipe is an ideal one to try out the grated frozen butter technique. Just freeze the butter and then grate it into the flour, combine quickly and top the apple mix.

Apple strudel

A delicious pudding from Austria but popular all over Northern Europe. Strudel comes from the German word for whirlpool, because the curling pastry resembles such a thing. It's best served warm, not hot, with ice cream. Of course, strudels don't have to be sweet. In the Pfalz region of Germany they make *blutwurststrudel*, which sees potato added to the dough and a filling of bacon, sauerkraut and the local version of black pudding.

INGREDIENTS

- 375g of ready-made puff pastry
- 4 Bramley apples, peeled and cored
- Handful of sultanas
- 20g of ground almonds
- 10g of soft brown sugar
- 1 teaspoon of cinnamon
- 1 egg, beaten
- Drop of milk for brushing

Traditionally strudel pastry would be made from scratch and require long bouts of kneading to develop the gluten, but while this may be traditional it's also hugely time-consuming. So I've cheated a bit and used puff pastry that I've rolled even thinner. Filo would work too.

METHOD

1 Preheat the oven to 180°C.
2 Lightly oil a baking tray.
3 Prepare the apple. You need very thin slices that will cook quickly inside the pastry and not leach out loads of water making it soggy. Using a grater or a food processor, grate the apple into a sieve and then squeeze out any excess water. Add the almonds, sugar and cinnamon to the apple and combine.
4 Lay out a big sheet of baking parchment and lightly dust it with flour. Place the pastry on it and cut to 30cm x 20cm. Dust your rolling pin and roll the pastry a little flatter. Brush all four edges with the beaten egg.
5 With the longest edge facing you, spread the apple mixture over two-thirds of the pastry.
6 Using the edge of the baking parchment, start gently rolling up the pastry. Brush the final edge with a bit more egg to get a good seal and press together gently.
7 Put the strudel back in the fridge for 10–15 minutes to chill the pastry.
8 When ready to bake, brush the strudel with the remaining egg mixed with a little milk and dust over some caster sugar. Make a few slashes in the top of the strudel to let any steam out.
9 Place on the greased baking tray with the seam of the strudel underneath, and bake in the oven for 20–25 minutes until golden brown.

Note: Alternatively you can chop the apple pieces larger and soften them in a pan with a little butter. You still want them to have a little bite, mind you, and remember they'll continue cooking in the oven. Other fruits, both tinned and fresh, can be used in this recipe. Just make sure you've removed as much moisture as you can to keep the pastry from going soggy.

Bread and butter pudding

Bread and butter pudding is one of a European-wide family of dishes that pairs leftover bread with egg or cream (*pain perdu* in France is another, and similar to our eggy bread, also known as poor knights of Windsor).

INGREDIENTS

(Serves 4–6)

- Half a brioche loaf, slightly stale
- Handful of dried raisins
- 200g of butter at room temperature
- 300ml of custard (made as instructed on page 57)
- 200ml of double cream
- Nutmeg

It's been known in the UK since the 1700s. Of course, today we play fast and loose with the whole idea of the bread element, and I've seen recipes that use old hot cross buns, tea cakes and even croissants. If you really want to gild the lily (and who doesn't like gold-plated flowers once in a while?), you can't beat brioche. It's sweet, has a lovely golden colour, and is easily soft enough to soak up the custard and give a good wobble without disintegrating to pieces.

Now you *can* make your own brioche from scratch, but let's be honest, it's a bit of a faff, especially as you're going to drown it in custard and sugar. What I sometimes do is make one in the bread maker, let it go firm for a few days somewhere cool and dry, and then use that. Alternatively just buy one. You should definitely make your own custard, however. I've added a handful of plump raisins too, but you could get creative with all sorts of extras – slices of fruit, marmalade instead of butter, caramel or chocolate chips, and so on.

METHOD

1 Preheat the oven to 160°C.
2 First, butter the brioche and cut diagonally into triangles. Butter a rectangular ceramic dish and arrange the slices alternately with a bit of room between each. Scatter the raisins over them.
3 Make the custard as described on page 57 and let cool slightly.
4 Add the double cream to the made custard and pour over each slice of brioche.
5 Wiggle the slices around using a spatula to ensure all the custard gets between each one – there should be no dry bread bits. Leave to soak for 20 minutes. (You can do all this in advance.)
6 Grate the nutmeg over the top and bake in the oven for 40–50 minutes or until the custard has set to a good wobble.
7 Remove and leave to cool. You want to serve it warm rather than piping hot. Dust with a little icing sugar prior to serving.

Syrup sponge pudding

One of the simplest puds in this book, a union of sponge and golden syrup. Takes a while to cook, mind, but it's an absolute crowd-pleaser for all the family. I tend to dial down the sweetness in the sponge mix, as you've got plenty of gob-stopping sweetness from the syrup.

INGREDIENTS
- Six tablespoons (around 100ml) of golden syrup
- 170g of unsalted butter at room temperature plus a little extra for greasing
- 100g of soft brown sugar
- Pinch of salt
- 3 eggs, beaten
- 175g of self-raising flour
- Milk
- Drizzle of golden syrup to serve, along with custard

One tiny piece of advice: this is best made in a 900ml/1½ pint reusable plastic pudding basin, which comes with a lid. It's a lot easier than all that folding, pleating and tying off of various papers on the top of a ceramic one.

METHOD

1 First check the size of your saucepan to pudding basin. You want a deep saucepan or stock pot with a heatproof saucer or trivet in the bottom. There should be enough height to the saucepan to allow the water to come halfway up the side of the pudding basin when it's placed on the saucer. It's a lot easier to judge all this first when everything's empty and cold. Once that's all sorted, crack on.

2 Grease the pudding basin lightly with some butter, and pour in the golden syrup so it settles on the bottom.

3 In a stand mixer or a bowl, beat together the butter, salt and the sugar until light and fluffy. Gradually add the eggs and combine before folding in the flour. Add enough milk to make a dropping consistency.

4 Spoon this into the pudding basin – stop around 3cm from the top. Place the plastic lid on.

5 Place the pudding basin on the saucer in the saucepan and fill with cold water. Bring up to just above a simmer and check the water level regularly (use a lid if your pan's tall enough), as you don't want it to boil dry.

6 Steam for 2 hours.

7 Turn off the hob and lift the basin out of the water. Remove the lid and let it stand for 5 minutes. Run a flat-bladed knife or palette knife around the edge of the pudding. Place a large plate on top and turn upside down. Give the basin a squeeze and a knock to loosen the pud. Drizzle over a bit more syrup if you like. Serve immediately.

Sticky toffee pudding

Sticky toffee pudding, or STP, appears on pub and restaurant menus all over the UK, and how well it's made is a good indication of how skilled the person in the kitchen is. A bad STP is a disheartening, strangely dry and decidedly 'unsticky' experience. The ultimate indication, however, is have they included the dates? These are critical for that rich, sticky, chewy interior, and it's a poor, lazy chef that omits them.

INGREDIENTS
(Serves four)
- 170g of dates (chopped, stones removed)
- 100ml of hot water
- 1 teaspoon of vanilla extract
- 60g of butter
- 170g of soft brown sugar
- 225g of plain flour
- 1 tablespoon of baking powder
- 1 teaspoon of bicarbonate of soda
- 1 beaten egg
- 1 tablespoon of treacle (optional, just ramps up the stickiness a bit)

For the toffee sauce
- 60g of brown sugar
- 2 tablespoons of double cream
- 1½oz (40g) of butter

The true creator of the STP was a Canadian friend of Patricia Martin, who lived in The Old Rectory, Claughton, Lancashire. Chef Francis Coulson, the original owner of the Sharrow Bay hotel in Cumbria, got hold of the recipe and adapted it slightly. He also helped popularise the dish. Francis' restaurant first opened its doors in 1948. It was the first of what we'd now think of as a country house hotel.

Another maker of STPs in the region is Cartmel, founded by Jean and Howard Johns. They took over the Cartmel village shop in 1989 and started baking cakes, including STP, for it to sell. Their cakes are now available in most supermarkets, and they've expanded the range to include sticky banana pudding and sticky ginger pudding amongst other things.

METHOD

1 Pour the hot water over the chopped dates first – this will rehydrate them. Add the vanilla extract and leave for 20 minutes. While they're coming round, line a square cake tin with baking parchment and grease well. Preheat oven to 160°C.

2 Place the butter and the sugar in the mixing bowl and cream together using a paddle on a stand mixer, or by hand. Sift in the flour and add the baking powder and bicarbonate of soda, then the egg, then the dates and the treacle if using. Make sure it's all well combined.

3 Pour into the cake tin and smooth over.

4 Bake in the oven for around 40 minutes, or until a stick inserted into the cake comes out clean. Let the cake cool before serving – you want it warm, not scalding hot.

5 You can serve with cream, or custard if you like, but toffee sauce is best. Add the butter and the sugar to a small pan and melt for a few minutes until caramelised, then stir in the cream and pour over the portions of cake.

Queen of puddings

Like bread and butter pudding and eggy bread, queen of puddings is yet another historical pudding that makes use of old bread. As the late English pudding expert Mary Norwak said in her 1981 classic *English Puddings Sweet and Savoury*, 'It is difficult now to realise the important part that bread played in so many people's lives.' Indeed, for many people it formed a large part of their diet, therefore it was not to be wasted.

INGREDIENTS

(Serves 6–8)

For the base
- 400ml of full fat milk
- 100ml of double cream
- 50g of butter
- 110g of caster sugar
- 150g of breadcrumbs
- Zest of a lemon
- 220g of jam (I recommend damson)
- 5 egg yolks

For the meringue
- 5 egg whites
- 130g of caster sugar
- Teaspoon of cider or white wine vinegar

You can make these as individual puds in ramekins, but I think it's best made as one big whole one. You'll need a 2-litre oval, square or rectangular dish. A classic queen of puddings contains an eggy breadcrumb baked base, spread with jam and topped out with meringue. Needless to say, you'll need a stand mixer with a balloon attachment to make the meringue. An electric whisk might do OK, but I found the blades cut through rather than beat the egg whites. Or you could use a hand whisk in conjunction with a strong arm.

METHOD

1. Preheat the oven to 180°C.
2. Melt the butter in a large saucepan, add the milk and lemon zest and warm to blood temperature. In a separate bowl whisk the egg yolks with the caster sugar and gently add to the milk. Then add the breadcrumbs and stir until thickened.
3. Butter a 2-litre dish, pour the breadcrumb mixture into it, and bake in the oven for about 15 minutes until it's set but still a bit wobbly. Take out and leave to cool. Crank the oven up to 200°C.
4. In another saucepan or the microwave, heat the jam to make it runny then pour or spread over the baked breadcrumb mix and set aside.

Making the meringue

5. Take your mixing bowl and pour in the vinegar, swill around, and wipe out with a piece of kitchen roll. This will ensure the bowl is free of any grease. The acid will also help the meringue form.
6. Add the egg whites and caster sugar and beat until soft peaks. You can just smear the meringue on the top and dab it to form peaks, but for a more regal look pipe on with a piping bag to form a sort of crown.
7. Bake in the hot oven for about 10 minutes or until the meringue has set and turned a little golden.

Cherry batter puddings

In France this dish is known as *clafoutis* and comes from Limousin in the middle of the country. In the UK it's associated with Kent.

INGREDIENTS
(Serves 4–6)
- 350g of frozen dark cherries
- 2 eggs
- 90g of plain flour
- 70g of caster sugar
- 100ml of full fat milk
- ½ teaspoon of vanilla extract
- 40g of butter

Black cherries are the ones to use. Rather than buy fresh cherries for the few weeks they're available, and drive yourself mad pitting them, you can now buy very good, pitted frozen black cherries in supermarkets – use these. They're most likely not from Kent, however.

It's best served warm rather than straight from the oven hot or stone cold. *Crème fraîche*, custard, cream or ice cream are all good accompaniments, as is a glass of cherry brandy. Finally, you want to make this in a shallow ceramic dish, rather than a cake tin.

METHOD
1 Preheat the oven to 180°C.
2 Grease the dish with some of the butter, sprinkle some of the caster sugar in and swirl round so it sticks to the butter (this will caramelise during cooking and give the edge and bottom a nice crust). Tip out any excess sugar.
3 Beat the eggs and sugar together first in a large bowl or mixer, then add the flour, vanilla extract, milk and eggs.
4 Melt the remaining butter in a small pan and add to the batter.
5 Add the cherries to the batter and gently mix.
6 Pour the batter into the sugar-lined dish and bake in the oven for around 40 minutes until golden and risen. Test with a skewer to see if it's done.
7 Leave to cool slightly and dust with icing sugar just before serving.

Bakewell pudding

There are claims, counter-claims and rumours galore as to when, where and by whom this dish was created. What is fairly certain is that it was known in the district surrounding Bakewell from the mid-1800s. Most accounts centre on a Mrs Greaves, who ran the Rutland Arms in the town in the 1860s, and it's she who is generally credited with popularising the dish. Her great-great-great-grandson, Paul Hudson, has written a short book about the subject entitled *Mrs Ann Greaves of the Rutland Arms and the Bakewell Pudding*.

INGREDIENTS

- 300g of puff pastry (either shop-bought or make your own – see page 49)
- Two tablespoons of jam
- Candied peel (optional)
- 50g of flaked almonds
- 4 eggs plus 1 egg white
- 100g of melted butter
- 100g of sugar

There's a distinct difference between a traditional Bakewell pudding and a Bakewell tart. The latter is made with shortcrust pastry and seems to be a late 20th century invention, while the former is made with puff pastry. It's a homely looking sort of pud, always made as one large pudding rather than individually, with a puffed-up crust and rich custard centre. Eliza Acton has a recipe in her *Modern Cookery for Private Families* from 1845, where she rather snootily observes, 'This is a rich and expensive, but not a very refined pudding. A variation of it, known in the south as Alderman's pudding, is we think, superior.' 'Ark at 'er!

This recipe from 1837 comes from the personal cook book of Clara Palmer-Morewood of Alfreton Hall, some 17 miles from Bakewell. Her book is now in the Derbyshire Record Office, and within its pages you'll find not only recipes but medicinal and veterinary concoctions such as lip salve and 'a cure for dogs who are troubled with the snort'.

METHOD

1 Preheat the oven to 180°C.
2 Roll out the puff pastry and line a shallow 18cm pie dish. Spread the jam over the pastry, remembering to leave a gap at the edge. Scatter on flaked almonds and the candied peel if using. Place in the fridge while you make the egg topping.
3 In a bowl put the four eggs and the egg white. Add the melted butter and sugar and beat with an electric whisk until fluffy. Pour into the pie dish and bake in the oven for 25–30 minutes. Leave to set and cool before serving.

Rice pudding

Skin or no skin? There are two camps when it comes to rice pudding. Me, I'm a skin kind of chap. Of course, rice pudding comes in tins, pots and cartons these days, but those are a mere shadow compared to a proper rice pud.

Growing up, this was a popular tea-time pudding because it was cheap, easy to cook and filled you up. My sister and I used to stir in a blob of jam, mixing it in to make it even more sweet as well as pink.

Most cultures have a sweet baked rice recipe, but there's a purity to a rice pud in this country. Not for me the addition of cardamom pods, dried fruit or other fripperies. This is four-square proper British comfort food – you want a grate of nutmeg or a blob of jam at the most. Finally, remember rice can double in size as it cooks, so don't overfill the dish. A 2-litre dish should be enough to hold this.

INGREDIENTS

- 30g of butter
- 30g of golden caster sugar
- 100g of pudding rice
- 900ml of full fat milk
- 100ml of double cream

METHOD

1 Preheat the oven to 140°C.
2 Melt the butter and sugar in a saucepan and add the rice. Stir like you would a risotto to ensure each grain is coated. Then transfer to a shallow dish, add the milk and the cream, grate over a pinch of nutmeg, and gently bake in the oven for around 2 hours.
3 Serve warm, rather than 'from the oven' hot, with a blob of jam.

Cambridge burnt cream

You might think this is just an English version of a *crème brûlée*, perhaps because the name is a literal translation of the French dish. However, you'd be wrong. In England, this sugar-topped baked custard dish is synonymous with Trinity College, Cambridge, and the dish still appears occasionally on its menus.

INGREDIENTS

- 6 egg yolks
- 80g of caster sugar, plus extra for the topping (or vanilla-infused sugar if you've made some)
- 1 vanilla pod split and de-seeded
- 350ml of double cream
- 150ml of full fat milk

Legend has it that the recipe came from a country house in Aberdeenshire, and was offered to the Trinity kitchens around 1849 by an undergraduate and promptly rejected. Thirty years passes and the lowly undergraduate becomes a fellow. He presents the dish again and, surprise surprise, this time everyone says it's marvellous. But custard dishes like this were served in England long before then. Indeed, Trinity's own website says, 'The story that *crème brûlée* itself was invented at the College almost certainly has no basis in fact. But since the later nineteenth century there has been an association between the pudding known as "burnt cream" and Trinity College.'

The custard in a perfect Cambridge burnt cream should be made with less sugar, which is the opposite to a *crème brûlée*, because the sweetness as well as the crunchy caramel flavour comes from a thicker topping of melted and caramelised sugar, which should take a good wallop with the spoon to break.

METHOD

1. Preheat the oven to 150°C.
2. Split the vanilla pod and place the seeds and outer case in a bowl with the milk and cream to infuse for 20 minutes.
3. In a pan, heat the milk and the cream to a gentle simmer.
4. Remove the vanilla pod from the milk (dry and use to flavour sugar).
5. In a large glass bowl whisk together the egg yolks and the caster sugar.
6. Pour the cream over the eggs, whisking all the time until fully combined.
7. Pour this custard into ovenproof dishes, teacups or ramekins and place in a roasting tin.
8. Pour boiling water into the tin so it reaches halfway up the sides of your dishes.
9. Bake in the oven for 35 minutes until the custards have set. Remove and leave to cool, then place in the fridge.
10. All of the above can be done the day before.
11. When ready to serve, sprinkle each dish with extra caster sugar and using a small kitchen blowtorch (or indeed a large one from the shed) caramelise the sugar topping. Be careful not to let it burn.
12. If you're all out of blowtorches you can do it under a screaming hot grill but do keep an eye on it, as the sugar can turn on a sixpence.

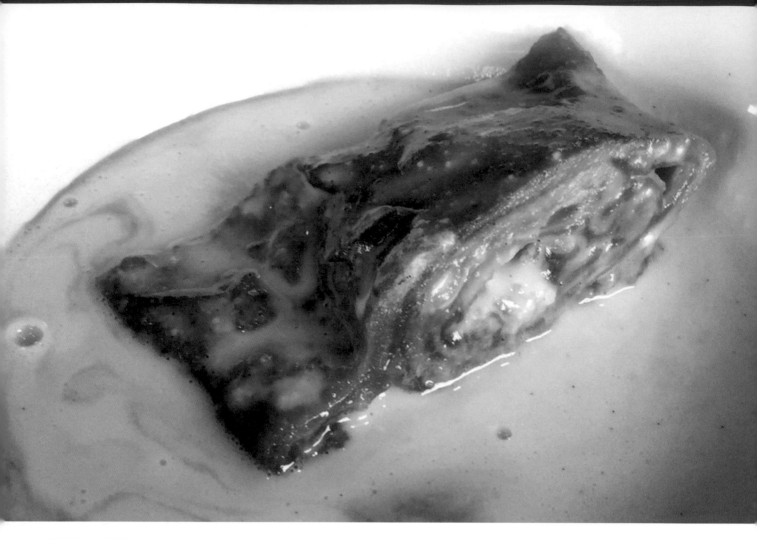

Hollygog

As English as tuppence and a real rib-sticker to boot, hollygog hails from Oxfordshire and was first made in the village of Kiddington. Being cheap and filling it was surely served at the colleges in Oxford.

INGREDIENTS
- 230g of plain flour
- 75g of butter
- 50g of lard
- A few tablespoons of cold water
- 4 tablespoons of golden syrup
- 250ml of full fat milk

It's essentially roly poly baked in milk, rarely seen on menus these days, but one place that serves it regularly is the Talbot public house in Knightwick, Worcestershire. There really is nothing better on a cold winter's day.

When you come to add the syrup make sure you've warmed it in a pan or the microwave, otherwise it won't spread very easily and might tear your pastry.

METHOD
1 Preheat the oven to 200°C.
2 Sieve the flour into a bowl and add the butter and the lard. Rub together quickly until it resembles fine golden breadcrumbs. Add the cold water until you form a stiff dough.
3 Dust your bench and roll the dough out into a rectangle about the size of a sheet of A4 paper. Brush your warmed syrup all over the dough and gently roll up the shortest side to make a cylinder.
4 Check the size against your baking dish – you want the hollygog to be a snug fit. Butter the dish well and place the hollygog in it. Put a few more dots of butter on the top of the dough and fill the dish with milk until halfway up the hollygog.
5 Place in the oven for around 45 minutes until golden. Slice and serve. You can make a custard using any milk remaining in the dish, or just serve it as it is as it'll be flavoured by the syrup.

Swiss roll

Despite the name, this classic British pud isn't Swiss in origin. The recipe book *Pot Luck: British Home Cooking* from 1914 says it's from Kent. It became more popular during the First World War, and indeed there are some references to its resemblance to a soldier's rolled-up kit.

INGREDIENTS

For the sponge
- 110g of caster sugar, plus extra for dusting
- 100g of self-raising flour
- 3 eggs
- Teaspoon of vanilla extract

For the filling
- 4 tablespoons of jam or marmalade

A variation on the Swiss roll is arctic roll, which was invented in the 1950s by a Czech émigré, Ernest Velden, and became immensely popular in the '60s and '70s. Nigel Slater, however, described it as 'tasting of frozen carpet', and it's perhaps a case of the actual reality trumping nostalgia.

You'll need a Swiss roll tin to make this, approx 20cm x 30cm. You also don't have to use jam. Why not try marmalade, or chocolate syrup, or some finely chopped nuts? Or you could play with the sponge, adding a tablespoon of cocoa to the mixture. Finally there's a bit of a knack to rolling the sponge. If for whatever reason yours ends in disaster (it shouldn't!), don't waste it, use it to make a trifle.

METHOD

1 Preheat the oven to 200°C.
2 Line the Swiss roll tin with baking parchment so it stands 3cm above the edge of the tin. You may need two pieces for this, one running left to right and one top to bottom. Lightly oil with vegetable or sunflower oil. Cut another piece of baking parchment 5cm larger than the Swiss roll tin, lay it on a clean tea towel, dust with a little of the caster sugar and set aside (you'll turn the baked sponge out on to this).
3 Cream the eggs and sugar together until pale and fluffy and tripled in volume. Add the flour using a sieve and continue to combine gently.
4 Pour the mixture into the Swiss roll tin. It won't look very deep but that's OK – remember, it'll puff up as it cooks.
5 Bake in the preheated oven for 8–12 minutes, until a very pale gold and springy to the touch (you can open the oven door and check after 8 minutes). Far better to underdo it than over.

6 Turn out the cooked sponge on to the waiting sheet of baking parchment and peel off the layer that was in the tin. Cut 1cm off all four edges (these will be the hardest bits and can hinder you rolling them up).
7 Turn the sponge so it's portrait in orientation, rather than landscape, and cut a shallow, thin groove, not all the way through, about 2cm in from the bottom edge nearest you.
8 Spread the jam on the sponge, leaving a 1cm border at each edge.
9 Take the edge of the baking parchment and roll the edge nearest you into the groove you've made. Continue to gently roll along the width of the sponge using the baking parchment as a guide. Be careful not to roll it into the sponge!
10 Leave sealed in the parchment, seam-side down and covered with the tea towel, until completely cold.

Jam roly poly

If the thought of tackling a Swiss roll gives you the heebie-jeebies, start with a jam roly poly. A 'JRP' differs from a Swiss roll in that it's made with suet pastry, rather than cake mix, and consequently it's a lot easier to roll than a baked sheet of sponge. In many ways it has more in common with the hollygog (page 164) than the Swiss roll, but one might think of these as all part of the same rolled pud tradition. Other members of this family include the roulade in France, which is made with meringue rather than cake mix, and apple strudel in Germany.

Adding currants to the dough and removing the jam gives you a spotted dick.

Once you've mastered the sweet version, why not try a savoury one? Mushrooms and bacon would be a good filling, along with some herbs and a grating of strong cheddar cheese.

INGREDIENTS
- 175g of self-raising flour
- 40g of light brown sugar
- Pinch of salt
- 75g of shredded suet (if vegetarian, use the veggie one)
- 6 or 7 tablespoons of cold water
- 5 tablespoons of good quality jam

METHOD

1 Preheat the oven to 190°C. Grease a 30cm x 20cm sheet of baking paper with a little vegetable oil. Cut a sheet of tin foil the same size.

2 Make the pastry by mixing together flour, salt, brown sugar and suet in a stand mixer fitted with a dough hook (alternatively, mix by hand). Add the cold water and combine until you've got a light, stretchy dough with no lumps in it.

3 On a floured surface roll the dough into an oblong shape around 20cm x 15cm.

4 Warm the jam a little in the microwave or a saucepan so it spreads easier, then pour on to the dough and brush around, leaving a 1cm gap around the edge. Brush this gap with a little milk.

5 Roll up longest edge to longest edge, and place on the greased baking paper with the seam on the underside. Roll the baking paper loosely around the roly-poly and then wrap the tin foil loosely around that, as the pastry will expand during cooking. Twist the ends to seal.

6 Place the roly poly on a wire rack above a roasting tin filled with boiling water. Ensure that it doesn't touch the water, however. Bake for 40 minutes. Remove and slice into discs and serve with custard.

Eve's pudding

An easy-to-make pudding that today sits somewhere between a crumble and a cobbler and is topped with a sponge cake-like mix. Prior to the invention of baking powder, however, it would have been made with breadcrumbs and boiled in a pudding cloth.

INGREDIENTS

- 450g of Bramley apples, peeled and cored
- 75g of soft brown sugar
- Juice and zest of a lemon
- 75g of butter
- 75g of caster sugar
- 1 egg, beaten
- 125g of self-raising flour
- Handful of flaked almonds
- Drop or two of milk

METHOD

1 Preheat oven to 160°C.
2 Zest the lemon and set aside then squeeze the juice into a bowl of water. Thinly slice the apples and place in the water to stop discolouration. Cream the butter and the caster sugar together until light and fluffy.
3 Grease an ovenproof dish lightly with butter and place the slices of apple in it. Sprinkle the brown sugar and the lemon zest over them.
4 Add the egg to the creamed butter and sugar, and then fold in the flour. Add a little mix to give you a dropping consistency.
5 Spread over the apple slices, scatter on the almonds and bake in the oven for about 45 minutes until the apples are cooked and the sponge golden. Serve with custard or cream.

Apple and rhubarb cobbler

Cobbler dough is actually more like a scone mix, and sits atop your filling allowing bits to peek out. It's pastry that can't quite be bothered to get itself together. You can make savoury or sweet cobblers – this one's sweet. What's more, I've added a little kick to the dough in the form of chopped crystallised ginger. These give a pleasant tang that works well with the rhubarb and soft apple.

INGREDIENTS

For the cobbler dough
- 225g of plain flour
- 4 teaspoons of baking powder
- 60g of caster sugar
- 100g of butter
- 2–4 tablespoons of milk
- Pinch of salt
- Handful of crystallised ginger roughly chopped

For the filling
- 3 sticks of rhubarb
- 2 Bramley apples, peeled, cored and chopped into large chunks
- 2 dessert apples, peeled, cored and chopped into smaller chunks

METHOD

1 Wash and chop the rhubarb into 3cm pieces. Peel the apples and chop into chunks. Place all the fruit in a saucepan on a low heat. Add 2 tablespoons of water or apple juice if you have some. Place the lid on – you want the fruit to steam and soften a bit.

2 After 10–15 minutes the fruit should have softened a little but still be holding its shape. Transfer to a ceramic dish and leave to cool. This can be done in advance and chilled.

3 Preheat the oven to 170°C.

4 To make the cobbler dough, sieve the flour and salt into a bowl, add the butter cut up into pieces and rub together with your fingers until it resembles golden breadcrumbs. Add the crystallised ginger and the salt. Add the milk and gently bring together to make a soft dough.

5 You can either just spoon this on to your filling, or transfer the dough to a floured work surface and gently roll out to about 2cm thick and cut out round with a pastry cutter or even a glass. These discs can then be placed on the filling. Personally I prefer the rough and ready approach.

6 Once you've applied the dough, get it in the oven as quickly as possible. Cook for around 20 minutes until the dough mix has expanded and become nicely golden. Serve with cream or custard.

Chocolate soufflé

For some reason soufflé scares even the most seasoned of home cooks. Many a host has crouched by the oven and offered up the silent prayer 'Please rise, please rise'.

There are a few tips to ensuring your soufflés come out standing proud and not a sunken eggy mess. Firstly, use a metal spoon to incorporate the rest of the beaten egg whites, and secondly never open the door while they're cooking. You'll need six ramekins for this recipe.

INGREDIENTS
- 20g of melted butter (for greasing)
- 60g of caster sugar
- 5 egg yolks, beaten
- 7 egg whites
- 175g of good quality dark chocolate (around 70% cocoa), broken into pieces
- Icing sugar for dusting

METHOD
1. Place a baking tray in the oven and preheat to 200°C.
2. Melt the butter in the microwave or a pan and brush the inside of each ramekin with the butter. Add a large tablespoon of the caster sugar to each one as you go and swirl around to ensure the sugar sticks to the melted butter and the insides of each ramekin are coated in sugar. This should use about 10g of it.
3. Place the chocolate in a bowl above a pan of simmering water (ensuring it does not touch it) and melt.
4. Add the eggs and the remaining caster sugar to the melted chocolate and combine.
5. Using a balloon attachment whisk the egg whites until they form soft peaks. Using a metal spoon add a spoonful of the beaten egg white to the chocolate mix and very gently combine.
6. Add the rest of the egg white until just combined.
7. Portion out into each ramekin, you want each about three-quarters full. Run a piece of kitchen roll around the lip and just inside each ramekin to ensure they are clean and free of any loose chocolate mix – this should ensure a straight rise.
8. Place on the baking tray and bake for 10 minutes; do not open the door. After 10 minutes open the oven door and check the soufflés. They should have a slight wobble.
9. Remove and dust with a little icing sugar and serve.

Baked Alaska

What's not to love about baked Alaska? This retro pud is a history and science lesson in cake form! First the history. US President Thomas Jefferson reputedly ate a dish of ice cream encased in pastry at a banquet in 1802, but it wasn't the dish we now know as baked Alaska. A near identical dish featuring meringue over ice cream but called *omelette à la Norvégienne* was invented just two years later, again in the USA.

INGREDIENTS

- 1 tub of good quality vanilla ice cream
- 2 eggs, their weight in unsalted butter, caster sugar and plain flour (or 110g of each)
- 1 teaspoon of vanilla extract
- 1 tablespoon of jam
- 3 egg whites
- 125g of golden caster sugar

The name baked Alaska didn't appear until 1876, when chef Charles Ranhofer at Delmonico's Restaurant in New York City did a version of the dish to commemorate the United States' purchase of the territory of Alaska in 1867. The cost of this huge piece of land (over 580,000 square miles) was a mere $7.2 million ($121 million in 2015), which is a bargain really. As Mark Twain once said, 'buy land, they've stopped making it'.

As for the science, well the reason the ice cream doesn't melt is that the air trapped in the meringue acts as an insulating foam protecting the ice cream from the heat. The trick is to go from the depths of the freezer to an oven at full whack for just enough time to lightly brown the meringue.

Like most recipes in this book, you can tweak some of the flavourings and ingredients. The recipe below is for a vanilla baked Alaska, quite literally. But you could make it more exciting and opt for chocolate sponge, whisky marmalade and Bailey's flavoured ice cream.

Now of course, a baked Alaska is one of those puds that you can make entirely from scratch, including the ice cream. And if you do, bravo! However, that takes a lot more time than making a sponge and whipping a few egg whites. Consequently I've cut a corner here and bought ice cream in.

A word on construction. You'll need one 20cm shallow Victoria sponge tin and a deep round bowl around 16cm across and 8–10cm high. You want at least 2cm between the edge of the sponge and the start of the ice cream – this is where your meringue will go.

METHOD

1 Preheat the oven to 170°C.
2 Take the ice cream out of the freezer and let it warm up a little so you can get a spoon in easily.
3 Line the deep bowl with cling film and smooth out as much as possible, leaving some hanging over the edge of the bowl (this helps you get the ice cream out later).
4 Scoop out ice cream with a tablespoon and pack into the bowl tightly.
5 Place back in the freezer to set hard again.
6 Place a cake tin on a piece of baking parchment and score round it with the tip of a very sharp knife. Grease and line your cake tin.
7 Place a bowl on the scales and reset to zero. Crack the eggs into the bowl and make a note of the weight.
8 Place another bowl on the scales and reset, weigh out the same weight of butter (or just go for around 110g) and cut into small cubes.
9 Place the butter in the bowl of a stand mixer, or if beating by hand leave in the bowl.
10 Weigh out the sugar and add to the butter. Mix until light and fluffy.
11 Add the eggs to the butter and weigh out the flour. Add this gradually too.
12 Add the vanilla extract and last of all the baking powder.
13 Place the mixture in the lined cake tin and smooth over with a spatula or palette knife.
14 Place in the oven and bake for 20 minutes.
15 Test with a metal skewer. If it comes out clean the cake is done.
16 Leave to cool for 5 minutes before removing from the tins and peeling off the baking parchment.

When the cake is cool enough to handle easily, place in the freezer.
17 All of the above can be done the day before. When you're ready to assemble your homage to American real estate negotiations do the following.
18 Ensure your mixing bowl, balloon whisk attachment, hands and worktop are clean as a whistle. To make sure the bowl is in peak condition, rub a little of the vinegar or some lemon juice on kitchen paper around the bowl and whisk to remove any trace of grease.
19 Place the egg whites in the bowl and whisk until they form soft peaks – that is, they can just hold together as a point before collapsing back down.
20 Whisk in the sugar, one spoonful at a time. You should have a glossy, shiny mixture. Set this aside.
21 Cut a rough circle of greaseproof paper and place on a small flat baking tray.
22 Place the sponge on the paper and spread the jam over it, leaving a 2cm border around the edge.
23 Take the ice cream out of the freezer, dip the bowl briefly into a bowl of hot water and pull gently at the cling film to loosen the ice cream dome. Place this on top of the jam.
24 Using a palette knife, spread the meringue around the ice cream in as smooth a dome shape as you can. Place back in the freezer for an hour.
25 Preheat oven to 220°C. If you've got an oven with a top element as well as fan, select that mode.
26 Put the Alaska straight from the freezer into the hot oven for 3–4 minutes until the top is just starting to brown. Serve immediately with the above historical facts.

Three Chimneys hot marmalade pudding

This recipe comes from Shirley and Eddie Spear, who own the Michelin-starred Three Chimneys restaurant on the Isle of Skye in Scotland. It's been on the menu ever since they opened there in 1985.

INGREDIENTS

- 150g of fine brown breadcrumbs
- 120g of soft brown sugar
- 25g of self-raising wholemeal flour (white self-raising would do)
- 120g of fresh butter, plus extra for greasing the bowl
- 8 tablespoonfuls of well-flavoured, coarse-cut marmalade (home-made is always the best)
- 3 large eggs
- 1 rounded teaspoonful of bicarbonate of soda plus water to mix

The marmalade should run throughout the pudding, giving it a rich, golden colour. At the Three Chimneys it's served with Drambuie-flavoured custard. It is, as Shirley says, 'ridiculously popular and very easy to make'. The key is good, sharp marmalade, made with Seville oranges. Shirley makes her own through the winter months. The recipe for that, however, she's keeping a secret.

METHOD

1 Butter a 3-pint pudding basin well. Place the breadcrumbs, flour and sugar in a large mixing bowl. Melt the butter together with the marmalade in a saucepan over a gentle heat. Pour the melted ingredients over the dry ingredients and mix together thoroughly. Whisk the eggs until frothy and beat gently into the mixture until blended together well.

2 Last of all dissolve the bicarbonate of soda in 1 tablespoonful of cold water. Stir this into the pudding mixture, which will increase in volume as it absorbs the bicarbonate of soda. Spoon the mixture into the prepared basin. Cover it with a close-fitting lid, or alternatively make a lid with circles of buttered greaseproof paper and foil, pleated together across the centre and tied securely around the rim of the basin.

3 Place the pudding basin in a saucepan of boiling water. The water should reach halfway up the side of the basin. Cover the pan with a close-fitting lid and simmer the pudding for 2 hours. The water will need topping up throughout the cooking period. Turn out on to a serving dish, slice and serve hot with fresh cream, ice cream, or – as they do at the Three Chimneys – with Drambuie custard.

INGREDIENTS

- 275ml of fresh milk
- 275ml of fresh double cream
- 6 egg yolks
- 100g of caster sugar
- 2 tablespoonfuls of Drambuie liqueur

DRAMBUIE CUSTARD

This is a proper egg custard flavoured with Drambuie liqueur. It's served warm, poured around the pudding. Alternative flavours could be added, such as vanilla, ginger or crushed cardamom, if you prefer. A tablespoonful of fresh ground coffee can be added, which is delicious with hot or cold chocolate desserts.

METHOD

1 Whisk the egg yolks together with the sugar until pale, slightly thick and creamy.
2 Gently warm the milk and cream until it's just beginning to bubble. Pour the milk and cream on to the egg and sugar mixture and whisk together. Return the mixture to the saucepan.
3 Bring to the boil very slowly, stirring all the time. As soon as it begins to thicken or coats the back of the wooden spoon, remove from the heat and pour into a bowl or jug for serving. Stir in the Drambuie or flavouring of your choice.
4 Serve immediately. Alternatively, cool the custard quickly in a bowl sitting on ice and refrigerate when cold until required. The custard can be used cold for assembling a trifle or serving with frozen or chilled desserts, or reheated carefully for serving with a hot pudding.

Lemon delicious pudding

This light, lemony pud doesn't look much, but after a spell baking in the oven it changes into something really special. You should end up with a creamy, eggy base and a light golden sponge on top. It's the sort of thing to serve after roast chicken on a warm, summery Sunday, when you want something for pud but don't want a bowling ball of heavy stodge in your stomach.

INGREDIENTS

- 100g of butter
- 125g of golden caster sugar
- Zest and juice of two unwaxed lemons
- 2 eggs, separated
- 300ml of milk
- 100g of self-raising flour

METHOD

1 Grease a 1¼ litre/2 pint dish. Cream the butter and sugar together with the lemon zest until pale and fluffy. Then add the egg yolks, half the milk, then the flour. Add the rest of the milk and the lemon juice. The mixture might look slightly curdled, but don't worry, that's normal.

2 In a spotlessly clean glass or metal bowl, beat the two egg whites to soft peaks and, using a spatula, fold into the mixture.

3 Pour into the greased dish and place a roasting tin in the oven. Fill the tin with water until it comes a third of the way up the side of the dish containing the sponge.

4 Bake for around 50–60 minutes until the top is golden and firm to the touch.

5 When done, allow to cool a little and dust the top with icing sugar.

6 Serve with cream or custard.

Clootie dumpling

Clootie dumpling comes from a time when few households in Scotland (or elsewhere in the UK, for that matter) had ovens, and most food was boiled in a pot over a fire. 'Clootie' is an old Scottish word for cloth, which was used to bundle up the pudding mix and hold all the ingredients together. This was then submerged in a large pot of boiling water to cook.

INGREDIENTS
- 125g of suet
- 125g of soft breadcrumbs
- 125g of self-raising flour, plus extra for dusting
- 50g of wholemeal flour
- 1 teaspoon of baking powder
- 250g sultanas, currants or a mixture of the two
- 100g of soft light brown sugar
- 1 teaspoon of ground cinnamon
- 1 teaspoon of ground ginger
- 1 teaspoon of ground nutmeg
- 1 teaspoon of allspice
- 2 tablespoons of golden syrup
- 4 tablespoons of milk to soften the mixture

(You can make breadcrumbs by blitzing up bread – just toast it a little first to dry it out.)

As for what's in the cloth, well, anything's fair game, though flour, breadcrumbs, currants, suet, eggs, sugar and spices such as cinnamon, nutmeg and ginger are present in various amounts. On the East Coast of Scotland treacle is sometimes used, leading to a much darker pudding. It's basically like a Christmas pudding.

There's a knack to making a good clootie. First you must boil the cloth. This not only makes sure it's clean, but after a good dusting of flour on it it also stops the pudding sticking. Then mix the dry ingredients together, moisten with a drop of milk and place on the cloth, which is tied up tight in a ball and slipped into the simmering hot water. After it was cooked it would sit in a dish by the dwindling fire to dry. You can, of course, do this in your oven.

It does take a little skill to make a good clootie properly and not end up with a cake-mix-covered cloth floating in hot water, and there are those who omit the 'clootie' altogether and steam the pudding mix in a bowl, but that's cheating.

METHOD
1 Gather and measure out all your ingredients. Put your largest saucepan on the stove, place an upside down saucer or trivet in the bottom an half-fill with water.
2 Boil a 50cm x 50cm piece of muslin for 3 minutes then remove from the pan. Squeeze out the excess water (careful, it will be hot).
3 Rub the suet into the breadcrumbs and add all the other dry ingredients including the fruit. Finally add the golden syrup and milk to soften a little. You want a stiffish, oozing consistency.
4 Dust the centre of the cloth with 2 tablespoons of flour.
5 Pile the mixture in the centre of the cloth and draw up the edges, leaving a little room for expansion, and tie the top with string.
6 Place in your large saucepan and top up with water if needed. Cover with a lid and turn on the heat. Bring to a rolling simmer and cook for 3½ hours, topping up the water if necessary.
7 Preheat the oven to 170°C.
8 Take the dumpling out of the water and refresh in cold water for a few moments. Remove the cloth and place on an ovenproof plate or dish, and place in the oven for 15 minutes to dry out.
9 Serve with lashings of custard.

Pavlova

The pavlova was invented in the 1920s to celebrate Russian ballerina Anna Pavlova's tour of Australia and New Zealand, and both countries now lay claim to owning the dish. The *Oxford English Dictionary* has now stepped in like some sort of culinary umpire, and ruled in favour of New Zealand.

INGREDIENTS

For the meringue
- 150g of egg whites
- 250g of caster sugar
- 4 teaspoons of cornflour
- 1 teaspoon of cider vinegar

For the filling
- 300ml of double cream
- Selection of prepared fruits and berries

In both countries, though, a 'pav' is a popular pudding at Christmas dinner, where, due to it being their summertime, a heavy British steamed pudding with custard and brandy butter might be a little too much.

Always crack and separate your eggs individually in a separate bowl, and transfer to the mixing bowl only when you're sure you've got just the egg white and no yolk or shell.

If you're after a truly authentic one, use exotic fruits such as passion fruit, star fruit, kiwi fruit or mango. If you're planning on using banana, toss in a little lime juice first to prevent discolouring.

METHOD

1 Preheat the oven to 120°C.
2 Line a baking tray with greaseproof paper.
3 Ensure your mixing bowl, balloon whisk attachment, hands and worktop are clean as a whistle. To make sure the bowl is in peak condition, rub a little of the cider vinegar or some lemon juice on kitchen paper around the bowl and whisk to remove any trace of grease.
4 Place the egg whites in the bowl and whisk until they form soft peaks – that is, they can just hold together as a point before collapsing back down.
5 Whisk in the sugar, one spoonful at a time. Finally add the cornflour and vinegar.
6 You should have a glossy, shiny mixture.
7 Take a dab of the mixture and dot the four corners of the baking tray and place your greaseproof paper on top. This will help to stick the paper to the tray.

8 Using a metal spoon, spoon the mixture on to the centre of the tray and gently shape into a circle with a shallow dip in the centre. Tap the spoon on the edge of the meringue to create little peaks around the edge.
9 Bake for 1 hour, until the meringue is completely dry to the touch, then switch the oven off.
10 Leave the meringue in the oven, with the door slightly ajar, until completely cold.
11 In a clean bowl, beat the cream until it too forms soft peaks. Spoon into the meringue case, and then top with the fruit. Add a final dusting of icing sugar if you think it needs it. Serve at once.

Of course, you can get creative with the whole pavlova format by adding extra flavourings to the meringue such as cinnamon or cocoa powder, and different toppings such as chocolate and cherries.

The history of Eton mess

If you'd like a meringue-based pudding a little closer to home than Australasia, then why not make Eton mess? It's a very similar combination of meringue, cream and fruit, only more messy, as the name suggests. Even the great Heston Blumenthal, who you'd think would break out the liquid nitrogen on a dish like this, once declared, 'What is so wonderful about this dessert is that it cannot be improved upon.'

INGREDIENTS

- One large or several smaller meringues broken into small pieces about the size of a new potato
- 250ml of double cream, whipped into soft peaks
- A selection of fruits and berries (red ones work best I find)

Something called Eton mess was apparently first sold in the sock (tuck) shop at the eponymous school in the 1930s. However, it featured bananas or strawberries mixed with ice cream. Meringue, it seems, was a later addition.

Interestingly, a pudding called 'Eton mess aux fraises' appears on the menu of a garden party given at Marlborough House, London, on 5 July 1893. The party was to celebrate the marriage of Prince George, the Duke of York, to Princess Mary of Teck, so it must have been known in late Victorian times.

Finally, another tale sees the creation of Eton mess attributed to a Labrador dog who sat on a picnic in the back of a car and squashed a rather ornate pudding. Of course, history does not record the name of said hound, nor what happened subsequently, and the rest of the details are sketchy.

The best thing about making your own meringues for this is that you can make them light and chewy, as well as tweak the sweetness and additional flavours. Shop-bought meringues are OK, but I find them far too sweet.

Eton mess is a great back-up pudding to make if you're trying to make a pavlova and things don't go quite as planned and your meringue case breaks in the oven. Remember, style it out at all times in the kitchen. This is not so much a recipe as a set of basic instructions.

METHOD

1 Loosely combine all the ingredients in a bowl and serve.
2 I have on occasion added a tablespoon of strawberry yoghurt, or a squeeze of fruit puréo; as I say, it's a very flexible dish and the sort of thing you can make easily with the egg whites left over from making, say, Portuguese tarts (page 136).

Of course, with a few minor tweaks – such as replacing the meringue with toasted oatmeal and adding a drop of whisky and honey – this becomes the Scottish dish Cranachan.

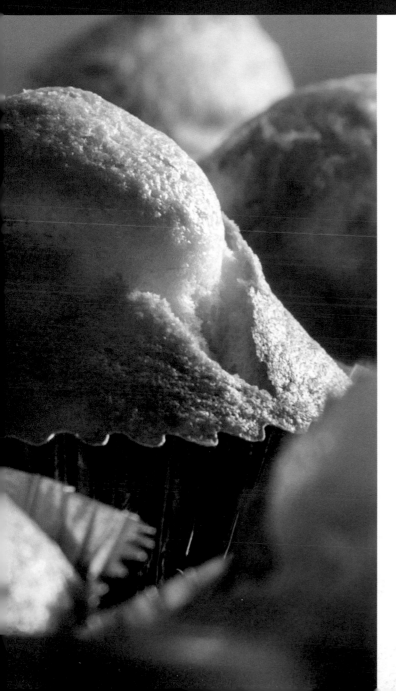

APPENDICES

TROUBLESHOOTING

USEFUL BITS

INDEX

Troubleshooting

Trouble loves to lurk in the kitchen, watching, waiting for that moment when you take your eye off the ball. Planning helps; before you start any recipe read through it – twice. Then spend some time assembling all the equipment you're going to need. Finally, get the ingredients out of the fridge and out of their packets, ready to be prepared.

Remember, no recipe is ever carved in stone. The recipes in this book are what worked for me, in my oven, on a particular day, with a particular set of ingredients. Don't think of them as rules. Instead, think of them more as a set of guidelines. Use your eyes, hands and nose to ascertain what's happing with your bakes; trust your instincts.

MY SPONGE CAKE HAS SPOTS ON THE TOP

This is caused by the butter being too cold and insufficiently whipped into the sugar. The little blobs of butter melt and leave a space under a very thin crust; this then burns.

MY CAKE'S RISEN UP AND CRACKED

Your oven's too hot. What's happening is that a hard crust is forming before the inside has had a chance to cook. When it expands, it hits the underside of the crust and bursts through it. Try baking at a lower temperature. The causes can be too much baking powder. If you're planning to ice or coat your cake, you could always cut off the protruding bit.

BOO, MY CAKE HAS SUNK IN THE MIDDLE

This can be for a few reasons, the main one being that the temperature in the oven was too low. Others include too much liquid and the cake getting knocked or moved during baking. Remember, never open the over door once the cakes are in.

MY CAKE HAS A GOOD TEXTURE BUT IS VERY FLAT

This is because you're using too big a cake tin. Remember, you want the raw batter mixture to fill the cake tin two-thirds full. For shallower sandwich cake tins you want it about 0.5cm from the lip of the tin.

MY CAKE IS STUCK IN THE TIN

Make sure you line your cake tin properly; also, if you're using wholemeal flours or ingredients like syrups these can cause it to stick. If you're making a fruit cake, always line the sides as well as the bottom of the tin.

MY BREAD HAS GONE ALL FLAT

This is probably due to the gluten not being developed enough and therefore not able to hold the structure together. It could also be because your dough is too wet.

MY BREAD IS RAW IN THE MIDDLE

Chances are the oven was turned up too high, so it looked done on the outside but the heat hadn't worked its way in. Try baking for longer next time, but turn the heat down a bit.

MY CHOCOLATE IS GRITTY

This happens when moisture has got into the pan. Even the tiniest drop can cause the chocolate to 'seize up' and turn grainy. Also, if you overheat chocolate it can turn thick and lumpy.

MY PASTRY IS TOO CRUMBLY

If you're making shortcrust and your pastry is too short, add a little more flour and work it a little. You don't want to knead it like bread dough, however. Also, make sure you've rested and chilled it for long enough.

MY PUFF PASTRY ISN'T PUFFED

Puff pastry needs to be cold and dry, and then go to a hot oven. This causes the butter to melt and produce steam, which raises the pastry. If puff pastry is warm, or touching a liquid filling, it'll never puff up, so keep it cold and as dry as possible.

MY TART CASE HAS SHRUNK IN THE TIN

Some shrinkage is inevitable, so pastry cooks and most chefs like to leave a few mm of pastry standing proud of the tin when they blind bake to allow for this. However, if yours has shrunk not only down the side but also contracted in the tin, either your pastry is overworked, by too much kneading or too much rolling, or it's had too much moisture. Remember to rest your pastry after forming together, and after rolling out and placing in the tin.

Useful bits

LAKELAND.CO.UK

This Cumbrian-based firm prides itself on its customer service and attention to detail. If you buy one of their own branded products it comes with a lifetime guarantee – even if the receipt has long since turned to dust. Consequently, they've been trusted by housewives, cooks and chefs for ages.

For many years they operated only via mail order, but they've now branched out into shops in major shopping areas, meaning you can examine and try a range of different products in store as well as have a chat with their knowledgeable staff. Their bakeware is excellent (it's what I use) and will last you forever.

KENWOOD

My favourite stand mixer manufacturer. There's a reason the original Kenwood Mixer is in the Design Museum – it's because their products are classics.

DELICIOUS.MAGAZINE

Every recipe in delicious. is tested and checked in the magazine's studio kitchen to make sure it not only works, but that it tastes amazing too. Go on, treat yourself to a subscription.

THE CAKE AND BAKE SHOW

Held at a variety of locations around the UK, and covering every aspect of baking, the Cake and Bake show is a great day out for any baking fan. There's normally a few *Great British Bake Off* contestants there showing their skills too.

Index

Acton, Eliza 160
Alderman's pudding 160
Alfreton Hall 160
all-in-one mixing method 35
apple cake recipe 92
apple crumble recipe 152
apple pie recipe 132–3
apple and rhubarb cobbler recipe 168
apple roses recipe 116–17
apple strudel recipe 153
arctic roll 165

baked Alaska recipe 170–1
baked cheesecake recipe 146
baker's dough scrapers 16
Bakewell pudding recipe 160–1
baking beads 18
baking parchment 18, 38–40
baking powder 28
baking problems 180–1
baking sheets 20
baking tins 20
balloon whisks 16
banana bread recipe 86
bannetons 20
Bath buns 112
Bath Olivers 112
beads 18
beef pie recipe 80–1
Beeton, Mrs 85
beetroot cake recipe 100
Berry, Mary 20
Bettys tearooms 107
bicarbonate of soda 28
biscotti recipe 125
bitter-sweet chocolate 58
blackberry tart recipe 144
blind baking 41
blowtorches 17
blueberry muffin recipe 126
blueberry tart recipe 144
Blumenthal, Heston 177
blutwurststrudel 153
boards (for chopping) 14
Bompas & Parr jellymongers 55
Book of Middle Eastern Food 97
bowls 17, 20
Bramley apples 92
brandy snap recipe 127

bread 8, 61
  making 30–4
  recipes 62–75
bread and butter pudding recipe 154
bread flour 25
bread knives 14
bread makers 20
bread recipes 62–75
brioche burger bun recipe 72
British buns 112
Brockett, John Trotter 127
brown loaf recipe 63
brown sugar 26
brownie recipe 128
brushes (for pastry) 15
buckwheat 25
buns of Britain 112
burger bun recipe 72
burnt cream recipe 163
butter 27
  recipe 70
buttercream 54

Cake and Bake show 181
cake decorating 17
  chocolate curls 59
cake levellers 17
cake mix 35, 37
cake tin liners 18, 40
cake tins 20
  greasing and lining 38–40
cakes 8–9
  making 37
  problems 180–1
  removing from tins 40
Cambridge burnt cream recipe 163
Carlyle, Thomas 112
carrot cake recipe 100
Cartmel village shop 157
caster sugar 26
Cavallari, Arnaldo 66
ceramic mixing bowls 20
chapati recipe 73
Charlotte (Queen) 112
cheesecake recipe 146
chef's knives 14
Chelsea bun recipe 110–11, 117
cherry batter pudding recipe 159
cherry pie recipe 134

chocolate 58
  gritty texture 181
chocolate cake recipe 96
chocolate chip cookie recipe 121
chocolate curls 59
chocolate éclair recipe 120
chocolate soufflé recipe 169
chocolate tart recipe 138
chocolate truffles 96
chopping boards 14
Chorley cake 129
Chorleywood bread process 34
choux pastry 46–7
  éclair recipe 120
  profiterole recipe 118–19
Christmas cake recipe 90–1
ciabatta recipe 66–7
clafoutis recipe 159
cling film 18
clootie dumpling recipe 175
cobbler recipe 168
coeliac disease 25
coffee and walnut cake recipe 89
Colorado Mine Company
  restaurant 75
cookie recipe 121
cooks' blowtorches 17
cornflour 25
Cornish apple cake recipe 92
Cornish scones 87
cornmeal flour 25
Coulson, Francis 157
couverture chocolate 58
cracked, hard cake crust 180
cream 56
creaming butter and sugar mixing
  method 35
crème anglaise 57
crème brûlée dishes 20
crème fraîche 56
Croquembouche 118
crumble recipes 152, 167
crumbly pastry 181
crumpet recipe 74
cupcakes 20
curd (lemon) 147
custard recipe 57
  Drambuie-URED 173
custard tart recipe 136

dark chocolate 58
dead fly pie recipe 129
decorating cakes 17
  chocolate curls 59
delicious. magazine 181
Delmonico's Restaurant 171
demerara sugar 26
desserts 9
Devon apple cake recipe 92
Devonshire scones 87
Dickens, Charles 134
digital scales 16
doors (to ovens) 13
Dorset apple cake recipe 92
double cream 56
dough scrapers 16
Drambuie custard recipe 173
dried yeast 28
dumpling recipe 175
dusters (for flour) 17

easy white loaf recipe 62
Eccles cake recipe 129
éclair recipe 120
electric whisks 16
English Food 112
English Puddings Sweet and Savoury 158
Eton mess recipe 177
Eve's pudding recipe 167
extra virgin olive oil 27

fan-assisted ovens 13
fat rascal recipe 107
fats 27
fig tart recipe 148
fingers (using) 41
flaky pastry 50–1
flan tins 20
flapjack recipe 113
flat bread recipe 73
flour 24–5
flour dusters 17
focaccia recipe 68
food processors 41
fool's gold loaf recipe 75
forks (for pricking the base) 18
fougasse recipe 69
fresh yeast 28
fruit tart recipe 144
fudge recipe 124

ganache 59, 96, 138
Gaskill, Mary 95
gingerbread recipe 108–9
Glasse, Hannah 101
Glossary of North Country Words 127

gloves 13
gluten-free flour 25
golden syrup 135
granary flour 25
Grand Marnier 127
granulated sugar 26
graters 16
greaseproof paper 18
greasing and lining tins 38–40
Greaves, Mrs Ann 160
Grigson, Jane 112
gritty chocolate 181
guides/rulers 17
gypsy tart recipe 142

Hand, Richard Gideon 112
hard, cracked cake crust 180
Heaton, Nell 95
hobnob recipe 114–15
hobs 13
hollygog recipe 164
hot cross bun recipe 106
hot marmalade pudding recipe 172–3
Hudson, Paul 160

icing recipe 91
icing sugar 26

jam roly poly recipe 166
jammy dodger recipe 122
Jefferson, President Thomas 170
jelly 55
Johns, Jean and Howard 157
jugs (for measuring) 15

Kennedy, Captain Jerry 75
Kent apple cake recipe 92
Kenwood stand mixers 19, 181
key lime pie recipe 143
Kilner-style jars 29
King Harry liqueur 97
kitchens 12
knives 14

Lakeland bakeware 181
Lancashire parkin recipe 95
Lancashire peelers 16
lard 27
Lékué silicone bread maker 20
lemon delicious pudding recipe 174
lemon drizzle cake recipe 93
lemon meringue recipe 147
lemon tart recipe 140–1
levellers 17
lime pie recipe 143
liners (for cake/loaf tins) 18, 40

lining and greasing tins 38–40
loaf tin liners 18, 40
loaf tins 20
  greasing and lining 38–40
Luyon, Solange 112
Lyle, Abram 135

making bread 30–4
making cakes 37
making pastry 41–51
malthouse flour 25
marmalade pudding 172–3
marzipan recipe 91
measuring jugs/spoons 15
meat pie recipe 80–1
melting chocolate 58
meringue recipe 52–3
  baked Alaska 170–1
  Eton mess 177
  lemon meringue 147
  pavlova 176
  queen of puddings 158
milk chocolate 58
milk pans 21
millionaire's shortbread recipe 105
mince pie recipe 137
mini tartlet tins 20
mitts 13
mixing 35, 37
mixing bowls 20
Modern Cookery for Private Families 160
molasses sugar 26
Mrs Ann Greaves of the Rutland Arms and the Bakewell Pudding 160
muffin recipe 126
muffin trays 20
muscovado sugar 26

Norwak, Mary 158
not crossed bun recipe 106

oil 27
Oliver, Dr William 112
omelette à la Norvégienne 170
orange and saffron cake 97
organic flour 25
oven gloves 13
ovens 13

pain perdu 154
palate knives 16
Palmer-Morewood, Clara 160
pane toscano 30
pans 21
parchment 18, 38–40
paring knives 14

parkin recipe 94–5
pasteis de nata recipe 136
pastry 9
  making 41–51
  problems 181
pastry blenders 41
pastry brushes 15
pâté brisée 44–5
pâté feuilletée 49
pavlova recipe 176
pear upside down cake recipe 98–9
pecan pie recipe 145
peelers 16
pie birds/funnels 17
Pietrafeso, Ron 75
pissaladiere recipe 78
pizza recipe 76–7
pizza stones 21
plain flour 25
plastic mixing bowls 20
plastic tubs/bowls 17
Portuguese custard tart recipe 136
Pot Luck: British Home Cooking 165
potato flour 25
pots and pans 21
Presley, Elvis 75
pricking with a fork 18
problem-solving 180–1
profiterole recipe 118–19
puddings 8–9
puff pastry 49
  not puffed 181
Pump Street Bakery (Orford,
  Suffolk) 129
pumpkin pie recipe 149

Queen Charlotte 112
queen of puddings recipe 158

raising agents 28–9
ramekins 20
Ranhofer, Charles 171
raspberry tart recipe 144
raw cakes 181
ready-made pastry 41
Real Bread Campaign 34
removable-bottom cake tins 20
removing cakes from tins 40
resting pastry 41
rhubarb and apple cobbler recipe 168
rice flour 25
rice pudding recipe 162
rocky road recipe 123
Roden, Claudia 97
rolling pastry 43

rolling pins 16, 43
  guide rings 17
roly poly recipes 164, 166
Royal Bun House 112
rulers/guides 17
Rutland Arms (Bakewell) 160
rye bread recipe 71
rye flour 25

saffron and orange cake 97
Sally Lunn buns 112
salted butter 27
saucepans 21
sausage roll recipe 79
savoury choux pastry 46
scales 16
scone recipe 87
Scott, Cindy and Buck 75
self-raising flour 25
semolina 25
serving spoons 15
Shallow Bay hotel 157
sharpening knives 14
shortbread recipes 104–5
shortcrust pastry 44–5
shrunken tart case 181
single cream 56
Slater, Nigel 89, 165
soda bread recipe 70
Somerset apple cake recipe 92
soufflé recipe 169
sour cream 56
sourdough loaf recipe 64–5
sourdough starters 29
spatulas 15
Spear, Shirley and Eddie 172–3
spelt flour 25
sponge pudding recipe 155
spoons 15
springform cake tins 20
stale bread 34
  recipes 133, 154, 158
stand mixers 19
starters 28–9
steamers 21
steels 14
sticky toffee pudding recipe 156–7
stockpots 21
storage
  of flour 24
  of starters 29
  of yeast 28
strawberry tart recipe 144
strong flour 25
strudel recipe 153

suet pastry 48
sugar 26
sunken cake middle 181
Swiss roll recipe 165
Swiss roll trays 20
syrup sponge pudding recipe 155

Talbot public house (Knightwick) 164
tarte au citron recipe 140–1
tarte Tatin recipe 139
tasting 12
Tate & Lyle 135
tea bread recipe 88
tea strainers 16
temperature 41
tempering chocolate 58
thermometers 13
Three Chimneys restaurant 172–3
thunder and lightning scones 87
tins 20
  greasing and lining 38–40
Toll House cookies 121
tongs 16
*Traditional Recipes of the British
  Isles* 95
treacle tart recipe 135
troubleshooting 180–1
truffles, chocolate 96
tubs 17
two knives method 41

unpuffed puff pastry 181
unsalted butter 27
upside down cake recipe 98–9

vegetable oil 27
vegetarian suet pastry 48
Velden, Ernest 165
Victoria sponge recipe 84–5

Wakefield, Ruth Graves 121
walnut cake recipe 89
wastage of bread 34
whetstones 14
whipping cream 56
whisks 16
white loaf recipe 62
wholemeal flour 25
wholemeal loaf recipe 63
work benches/worktops 12

yeast 28–9
Yorkshire Cookery Book, A 95
Yorkshire curd tart 146
Yorkshire parkin recipe 95